A
Digital Money
Ecosystem
Bitcoin Blockchain

DIPALI JADAV AND MANOJ KAMBER

 pencil

ISBN 978-93-5667-492-9
© DIPALI JADAV AND MANOJ KAMBER 2023
Published in India 2023 by Pencil

A brand of
One Point Six Technologies Pvt. Ltd.
123, Building J2, Shram Seva Premises,
Wadala Truck Terminal, Wadala (E)
Mumbai 400037, Maharashtra, INDIA
E connect@thepencilapp.com
W www.thepencilapp.com

Author biography

Dipali Jadav is a highly regarded author, researcher and expert in the field of digital currency and blockchain technology. With years of experience in the field, Dipali has earned a reputation as a thought leader and innovator. Her recently published book, "A Technology Digital Money Ecosystem: Bitcoin Blockchain", is a comprehensive guide to the rapidly evolving world of digital currency and blockchain technology. Through her research and expertise, Dipali provides readers with an in-depth understanding of the key concepts, technologies, and trends that are shaping the future of money and financial systems. The book is a must-read for anyone interested in the digital currency and blockchain space, offering insights and perspectives that are essential for staying ahead of the curve. Whether you are a seasoned expert or just starting to explore this fascinating and dynamic field, Dipali's book is a valuable resource that provides a clear and accessible overview of the key issues and trends. With her passion for the subject and her deep understanding of the technology and its applications, Dipali has truly made a significant contribution to the field of digital currency and blockchain. Her work has already been widely acclaimed and is sure to be a landmark publication in the years to come.

CONTENTS

1. Trust Making in Digital Transactions

It gives the idea that indeed, the innovative genie has been releasedfrom its jug. Called by an obscure individual or people withmuddled thought processes, at an unsure time ever, the genie is presently at ouradministration for one more kick at the can — to change the monetary power frameworkalso, the old request of human issues to improve things. On the off chance that we will it.Allow us to make sense of.The initial forty years of the Web brought us email, the Around the worldWeb, speck coms, virtual entertainment, the portable Web, huge information, distributed computing,what's more, the beginning of the Web of Things. It has been perfect for diminishingthe expenses of looking, teaming up, and trading data. It hasbrought the boundaries down to section for new media and diversion, new structuresof retailing and coordinating work, and extraordinary computerized adventures. Through sensor innovation, it has injected knowledge into our wallets, ourclothing, our vehicles, our structures, our urban communities, and, surprisingly, our science. Itis immersing our current circumstance so totally that soon we will no more"sign on" yet rather continue on ahead and our lives drenched inunavoidable innovation.By and large, the Web has empowered numerous positive changes — for thosewith admittance to it — however it has serious restrictions for business and financialaction.

5

The New Yorker could rerun Peter Steiner's 1993 sketch of onecanine conversing with one more without amendment: "On the Web, no one knowsyou're not kidding." On the web, we actually can't dependably lay out each other'spersonalities or trust each other to execute and trade cash withoutapproval from an outsider like a bank or an administration. These equivalentdelegates gather our information and attack our protection for business gainwhat's more, public safety. Indeed, even with the Web, their expense structure prohibits a few 2.5 billion individuals from the worldwide monetary framework. In spite of thecommitment of a shared enabled world, the financial and politicalbenefits have demonstrated to be unbalanced — with power and thrivingdiverted to the individuals who as of now have it, regardless of whether they're done procuring it.Cash is getting more cash than many individuals do.Innovation doesn't make success anything else than it annihilates security.Notwithstanding, in this advanced age, innovation is at the core of pretty mucheverything — great and awful. It empowers people to esteem and to disregard oneone more's rights in significant new ways. The blast in on the webcorrespondence and business is setting out additional open doors forcybercrime. Moore's law of the yearly multiplying of handling powercopies the force of fraudsters and cheats — "Moore's Outlaws"1 — not tonotice spammers, character cheats, phishers, spies, zombie ranchers,programmers, cyberbullies, and datanappers — lawbreakers who releaseransomware to keep information locked down — the rundown goes on. As soon as 1981, innovators were endeavoring to take care of the Web's concernsof protection, security, and incorporation with cryptography.

Regardless of how theyreengineered the interaction, there were dependably spills since outsiderswere involved. Paying with Visas over the Web was uncertainsince clients needed to unveil an excess of individual information, and the exchangecharges were excessively high for little installments.

In 1993, a splendid mathematician named David Chaum thought ofeCash, a computerized installment framework that was "an in fact wonderful itemwhich made it conceivable to securely and namelessly pay over the Web. . . .It was impeccably fit to sending electronic pennies, nickels, and dimesover the Internet."2 It was wonderful to the point that Microsoft and others werekeen on remembering eCash as an element for their software.3 The difficultywas, online customers couldn't have cared less about protection and security online then, at that point.Chaum's Dutch organization DigiCash failed in 1998.Around that time, one of Chaum's partners, Scratch Szabo, composed a shortpaper named "The God Convention," a contort on Nobel laureate LeonLederman's expression "the God molecule," alluding to the significance of the Higgs boson to current physical science. In his paper, Szabo pondered about themaking of a be-all end-all innovation convention, one that assigned God theconfided in outsider in all exchanges: "Every one of the gatherings wouldsend their contributions to God. God would dependably decide the outcomes andreturn the results. God being a definitive in confession booth watchfulness, noparty would learn much else about the other gatherings' contributions than theycould gain from their own bits of feedbacks and the output."4 His point was strong:Carrying on with work on the Web requires an act of pure trust.

Since thefoundation misses the mark on truly necessary security, we frequently have barely any choicehowever, to regard the brokers as though they were divinities.After 10 years in 2008, the worldwide monetary industry crashed. Maybefavorably, a pseudonymous individual or people named Satoshi Nakamotoillustrated another convention for a distributed electronic money framework utilizing acryptographic money called bitcoin.

Cryptographic forms of money (advanced monetary standards) areunique in relation to customary government issued types of money since they are not made orconstrained by nations. This convention laid out a bunch of rules — in thetype of dispersed calculations — that guaranteed the trustworthiness of the informationtraded among these billions of gadgets without going through a trustedoutsider. This apparently unpretentious demonstration set off a flash that has invigorated,panicked, or generally caught the creative mind of the processing scene andhas fanned out like quickly to organizations, state run administrations, security advocates,social improvement activists, media scholars, and writers, to name afew, all over the place."They're like, 'Wow, this is all there is to it. This is the enormous forward leap. Thisis what we've been sitting tight for,'" said Marc Andreessen, the cocreatorof the primary business Internet browser, Netscape, and a major financial backer ininnovation adventures. "'He tackled every one of the issues. Whoever he is ought toget the Nobel Prize — he's a virtuoso.' This is the thing! This is the conveyedtrust network that the Web generally required and never had."5Today insightful individuals wherever are attempting to comprehend theramifications of a convention that empowers simple humans to produce trustthrough shrewd code.

This has never occurred — confided in exchangesstraightforwardly between at least two gatherings, verified by mass cooperationalso, fueled by aggregate personal circumstances, instead of by huge organizationsinspired by benefit.It may not be the All-powerful, yet a dependable worldwide stage for ourexchanges is something extremely enormous. We're calling it the Trust Convention.This convention is the underpinning of a developing number of worldwideappropriated records called blockchains — of which the bitcoin blockchain isthe biggest. While the innovation is convoluted and the word blockchainisn't precisely resonant, the principal thought is straightforward. Blockchains empower us tosend cash straightforwardly and securely from me to you, without going through abank, a charge card organization, or PayPal.Instead of the Web of Data, it's the Web of Significant worth or ofCash. It's likewise a stage for everybody to realize what is valid — basically withrespect to organized recorded data. At its generally essential, it is an opensource code: anybody can download it free of charge, run it, and use it to createnew apparatuses for overseeing exchanges on the web. Thusly, it holds the potentialfor releasing innumerable new applications and at this point undiscovered capacitiesthat can possibly change numerous things. Large banks and a few states are carrying out blockchains asdispersed records to upset how data is put away andexchanges happen. Their objectives are praiseworthy — speed, lower cost, security,less mistakes, and the disposal of essential issues of assault and disappointment.These models don't be guaranteed to include a digital currency for installments.In any case, the most significant and broad blockchains depend onSatoshi's bitcoin model. This is the way they work.Bitcoin or other computerized cash isn't saved in a document some place; it'saddressed by exchanges kept in a blockchain — similar to a worldwidecalculation sheet or record, which use the assets of a huge sharedbitcoin organization to check and support each bitcoin exchange. Eachblockchain, similar to the one that utilizes bitcoin, is dispersed: it runs onPCs given by volunteers all over the planet; there is no focaldata set to hack. The blockchain is public: anybody can see it wheneversince it dwells on the organization, not inside a solitary establishment chargedwith examining exchanges and keeping records. What's more, the blockchain isscrambled: it utilizes rock solid encryption including public and confidential keys (rather like the two-key framework to get to a security store box) to keep up withvirtual security. You shouldn't for even a moment mess around with the frail firewalls of Target orHome Warehouse or a stealing staff member of Morgan Stanley or the U.S. governmentgovernment.At regular intervals, similar to the heartbeat of the bitcoin network, all theexchanges led are confirmed, cleared, and put away in a block which isconnected to the former block, in this manner making a chain. Each block mustallude to the first block to be legitimate.

This design forever timestamps and stores trades of significant worth, keeping anybody from adjusting therecord. If you had any desire to take a bitcoin, you'd need to change the coin'swhole history on the blockchain without really trying to hide. That is basicallyincomprehensible. So the blockchain is a dispersed record addressing an organizationagreement of each and every exchange that has at any point happened. Like the Around the worldWeb of data, it's the Overall Record of significant worth — a conveyedrecord that everybody can download and run on their PC.A few researchers have contended that the development of twofold passageaccounting empowered the ascent of private enterprise and the country state. This newcomputerized record of financial exchanges can be customized to recordessentially all that of significant worth and significance to humanity: birth and passingauthentications, marriage licenses, deeds and titles of proprietorship, instructivedegrees, monetary records, operations, protection claims, votes,provenance of food, and whatever else that can be communicated in code.The new stage empowers a compromise of computerized records with respect tobasically everything continuously. Before long billions of shrewd things in, as a matter of factthe actual world will detect, answering, imparting, purchasingtheir own power and sharing significant information, doing everything fromsafeguarding our current circumstance to dealing with our wellbeing. This Web ofEverything needs a Record of Everything. Business, trade, and theeconomy need a Computerized Retribution.So for what reason would it be advisable for you to mind? We accept reality can liberate us andappropriated trust will significantly influence individuals in varying backgrounds. Perhapsyou're a music sweetheart who believes craftsmen should get by off their specialty. Or on the other hand abuyer who needs to know where that cheeseburger meat truly came from.Maybe you're a worker who's tired of paying huge expenses to send cashhome to friends and family in your tribal land. Or on the other hand a Saudi lady who needs todistribute her own design magazine. Perhaps you're a guide specialist who requirements to recognize land titles of landowners so you can revamp their homes after antremor. Or on the other hand a resident tired of the absence of straightforwardness andresponsibility of political pioneers. Or on the other hand a client of virtual entertainment who valuesyour security and thinks every one of the information you produce may merit something—to you. Indeed, even as we compose, pioneers are building blockchain-basedapplications that serve these finishes. Also, they are only the start. Without a doubt, blockchain innovation has significant ramifications for someestablishments. Which makes sense of all the energy from many savvy andpersuasive individuals. Ben Lawsky quit his place of employment as the administrator ofmonetary administrations for New York State to assemble a warning organization in thisspace. He told us, "In five to a decade, the monetary framework might beunrecognizable . . . what's more, I need to be essential for the change."6 Blythe Experts,previously CFO and head of Worldwide Items at JPMorgan's speculation bank, sent off a blockchain-centered innovation startup to change the business. The front of the October 2015 BloombergMarkets highlighted Experts with the title "Everything revolves around theBlockchain." Moreover, The Financial expert ran an October 2015 main story,"The Trust Machine," which contended that "the innovation behind bitcoincould change how the economy works."7 To The Business analyst, blockchaininnovation is "the extraordinary chain of being certain about things."

Bankswherever are scrambling high level groups to explore valuable open doors,a portion of these with many crackerjack technologists. Brokers love thethought of secure, frictionless, and moment exchanges, yet some recoil at thethought of transparency, decentralization, and new types of money.

Themonetary administrations industry has as of now rebranded and privatized blockchaininnovation, alluding to it as conveyed record innovation, trying toaccommodate the best of bitcoin — security, speed, and cost — with a totallyshut framework that requires a bank or monetary establishment's consent touse. To them, blockchains are more solid information bases than what theyas of now have, information bases that empower key partners — purchasers, venders,caretakers, and controllers — to keep shared, permanent records, in this manner lessening cost, alleviating settlement risk, and dispensing with main issues ofdisappointment.Putting resources into blockchain new companies is taking off, as did putting resources into dotcoms during the 1990s. Financial speculators are showing energy at a levelthat would make a 1990s website financial backer blush. In 2014 and 2015 alone,more than $1 billion of investment overflowed into the arisingblockchain environment, and the pace of speculation is nearly multiplyingyearly.8 "We're very sure," said Marc Andreessen in a meetingwith The Washington Post, "that while we're staying here in 20 years, we'llbe discussing [blockchain technology the manner in which we discuss the Webtoday."Controllers have additionally snapped to consideration, laying out teams toinvestigate what sort of regulation, if any, appears to be legit. Dictatorstate run administrations like Russia's have restricted or seriously restricted the utilization ofbitcoin, as have majority rule expresses that ought to know better, similar to Argentina,given its set of experiences of money emergencies. More smart state run administrations in theWest are putting significantly in grasping how the new innovationcould change not just focal banking and the idea of cash, yet additionallygovernment activities and the idea of a vote based system. Carolyn Wilkins, thesenior representative legislative head of the Bank of Canada, trusts it's the ideal opportunity for focalbanks wherever to concentrate on the ramifications of moving whole trulypublic cash frameworks to computerized cash.

The Bank of Britain's topfinancial expert, Andrew Haldane, has proposed a public computerized cash forthe Assembled Kingdom.These are powerful times. Undoubtedly, the developing crowd of devoteeshas its portion of go getters, examiners, and crooks. The primary story mostindividuals catch wind of advanced monetary forms is the liquidation of the Mt. Goxtrade or the conviction of Ross William Ulbricht, pioneer behind the SilkStreet darknet market held onto by the Government Agency of Examination fordealing unlawful medications, youngster sexual entertainment, and weapons utilizing the bitcoinblockchain as an installment framework. Bitcoin's cost has vacillated definitely,furthermore, the responsibility for is as yet focused. A recent report showedthat 937 individuals claimed half of all bitcoin, albeit that is evolving today. How would we get from pornography and Ponzi plans to thriving? To start,it's not bitcoin, the still speculative resource, that ought to intrigue you, except if you're a broker. This book is tied in with an option that could be greater than the resource. It'sabout the power and capability of the hidden mechanical stage.It is not necessarily the case that bitcoin or cryptographic forms of money as such areinsignificant, as certain individuals have recommended as they scramble todisassociate their tasks from the outrageous endeavors of the past. Thesemonetary standards are basic to the blockchain upheaval, which is first andpremier about the shared trade of significant worth, particularly cash.

Trust in business is the assumption that the other party will actas indicated by the four standards of respectability: genuineness, thought,responsibility, and straightforwardness.Genuineness isn't simply a moral issue; it has turned into a monetary one. Tolay out confiding in associations with workers, accomplices, clients,investors, and the general population, associations should be honest, exact, andcomplete in correspondences. No lying through exclusion, no confusionthrough intricacy.Thought in business frequently implies a fair trade of advantages ordisservices that gatherings will work with sincere intentions. However, trust requires acertifiable regard for the interests, wants, or sensations of others, and thatgatherings can work with generosity toward each other.Responsibility implies sincerely committing to partners andcomplying with them. People and organizations the same should show thatthey have regarded their responsibilities and possessed their messed up guarantees,ideally with the confirmation of the actual partners orautonomous external specialists. No shifting responsibility elsewhere, no playing the faultgame.Straightforwardness implies working out in the open, in the radiance of day."What are they stowing away?" is an indication of unfortunate straightforwardness that prompts doubt.Obviously, organizations have real privileges to exchange insider facts and different sortsof restrictive data. However, with regards to appropriate data forclients, investors, representatives, and different partners, dynamicreceptiveness is integral to acquiring trust. As opposed to dressing for progress,organizations can strip down for progress.Trust in business and different establishments is generally at an untouched low. Theadvertising organization Edelman's 2015 "Trust Indicator" shows thattrust in establishments, particularly organizations, has fallen back to levels fromthe terribly low time of the 2008 extraordinary downturn. That's what edelman noticedindeed, even the once secure innovation industry, still the most trustedbusiness area, saw decreases in most of nations interestingly.All around the world, Presidents and government authorities keep on being the most un-dependabledata sources, falling a long ways behind scholar or industry experts.13Likewise, Gallup revealed in its 2015 overview of American trust inorganizations that "business" positioned second most minimal among the fifteenorganizations estimated; less than 20% of respondents demonstrated theyhad significant or elevated degrees of trust.

Just the U.S. Congress had a lowerscore.In the preblockchain world, trust in exchanges got frompeople, go-betweens, or different associations acting with trustworthiness.Since we frequently can't have the foggiest idea about our counterparties, not to mention whether theyhave honesty, we've come to depend on outsiders not exclusively to vouch foroutsiders, yet in addition to keep up with exchange records and play out the businessrationale and exchange rationale that powers trade on the web. These strongdelegates — banks, states, PayPal, Visa, Uber, Apple, Google,what's more, other computerized aggregates — gather a large part of the worth.In the arising blockchain world, trust gets from the organization andindeed, even from objects on the organization. Carlos Moreira of the cryptographicsecurity organization WISeKey said that the new innovations actuallydelegate trust — even to actual things.

"On the off chance that an item, whether it be a sensor on an interchanges tower, a light, or a heart screen, isn't trusted to perform well or pay for administrations it will be dismissed by different articles automatically."15 The actual record is the groundwork of trust.16All things considered, "trust" alludes to trading labor and products and to the honesty and security of data, not trust in all business undertakings. Nonetheless, you will peruse all through this book how a worldwide record of honest data can assist with incorporating trustworthiness into every one of our foundations and make a safer and more reliable world. In our view, organizations that direct some or each of their exchanges on the blockchain will partake in a trust knock in share cost. Investors and residents will generally expect all public firms and citizen-subsidized associations to run their depositories, at least, on the blockchain. In view of expanded straightforwardness, financial backers will actually want to see whether a President truly merited that fat reward.

Shrewd agreements empowered by blockchains will require counterparties to submit to their responsibilities and citizens will actually want to see whether their agents are telling the truth or acting with financial trustworthiness.

2. Internet Age

The principal period of the Web began with the energy and soul of a youthfulLuke Skywalker — with the conviction that any youngster from a cruel desert planetcould cut down a shrewd domain and begin another development by sending off awebsite. Gullible certainly, however many individuals, present organization included,trusted the Web, as epitomized in the Internet, would disturb themodern reality where power was grasped by the meager few and power structureswere difficult to climb and harder to overturn. Not at all like the old media that wereconcentrated and constrained by strong powers, and where the clients werelatent, the new media were appropriated and unbiased, and everybody was andynamic member as opposed to a uninvolved beneficiary. Minimal expense and monstrousdistributed correspondence on the Web would help subvertcustomary orders and help with the consideration of creating worldresidents in the worldwide economy. Worth and notoriety would get fromnature of commitment, not status. In the event that you were shrewd and focused inIndia, your legitimacy would bring you notoriety. The world would be compliment,more meritocratic, more adaptable, and more liquid. Generally significant,innovation would add to thriving for everybody, not only abundance forthe meager few.A portion of this has happened. There have been mass coordinated effortslike Wikipedia, Linux, and Cosmic system Zoo. Re-appropriating and arrangedplans of action have empowered individuals in the creating scene to partakein the worldwide economy better. Today two billion individuals team up as friendssocially. We as a whole approach data in phenomenal ways.Nonetheless, the Realm struck back. It has become evident that concentratedpowers in business and government have twisted the first fairengineering of the Web to their will.Colossal organizations presently control and own this new method for creationfurthermore, social communication — its fundamental foundation; huge and developinggold mines of information; the calculations that undeniably administer business andday to day existence; the universe of applications; and unprecedented arising abilities,AI, and independent vehicles. From Silicon Valley and WallRoad to Shanghai and Seoul, this new gentry utilizes its insider advantageto take advantage of the most phenomenal innovation at any point contrived to enableindividuals as financial entertainers, to construct marvelous fortunes and fortify itspower and impact over economies and social orders.

A large number of the clouded side worries raised by early computerized pioneers havebasically materialized.17 We have development in GDP yetnot similar work development in most evolved nations. We havedeveloping abundance creation and developing social imbalance. Stronginnovation organizations have moved a lot of action from the open,disseminated, populist, and enabling Web to shut online wallednurseries or restrictive, read-just applications that in addition to other things killthe discussion. Corporate powers have caught a considerable

19

lot of these greatshared, vote based, and open advancements and are utilizing them toremove an unreasonable portion of significant worth.The end result is that, regardless, monetary power has gotten spikier,more focused, and more dug in. As opposed to information being moregenerally and fairly appropriated, it is being stored and taken advantage of byless elements that frequently use it to control more and secure more power. Ifyou collect information and the power that accompanies it, you can furtherinvigorate your situation by creating restrictive information. This honorbests merit, no matter what its starting point.Further, strong "computerized aggregates" like Amazon, Google,Apple, and Facebook — all Web new companies all at once — are catching thegold mines of information that residents and foundations create frequently in privateinformation storehouses as opposed to Online. While they make incredible incentive forcustomers, one consequence is that information is turning into another resource class — one thatmay best past resource classes. Another is the sabotaging of ourcustomary ideas of security and the independence of the person.Legislatures of numerous sorts utilize the Web to further develop tasks andadministrations, yet they currently likewise convey innovation to screen and evencontrol residents. In numerous popularity based nations, legislatures usedata and interchanges advances to keep an eye on residents, changepopular assessment, further their parochial advantages, sabotage privileges andopportunities, and by and large to remain in power. Severe state run administrations like thoseof China and Iran encase the Web, taking advantage of it to get serious aboutcontradict and prepare residents around their targets.It is not necessarily the case that the Internet is dead, as some have proposed. TheWeb is basic to the fate of the advanced world and we all ought to helpendeavors under method for shielding it, like those of the InternetEstablishment, who are battling to keep it open, nonpartisan, and continuallydeveloping.Presently, with blockchain innovation, a universe of additional opportunities hasopened up to switch this multitude of patterns. We presently have a genuine distributedstage that empowers the many energizing things we've talked about in thisbook. We can each possess our characters and our own information. We can doexchanges, making and trading esteem without strongmediators going about as the authorities of cash and data. Billions ofbarred individuals can before long enter the worldwide economy.

We can safeguard ourprotection and adapt our own data. We can guarantee that makers aremade up for their protected innovation. As opposed to attempting to tackle theissue of developing social imbalance through the reallocation of richesno one but, we can begin to meaningfully have an impact on how abundance is appropriated — the way things are madein any case, as individuals wherever from ranchers to performers can shareall the more completely, deduced, in the abundance they make. The sky is by all accounts thelimit.It's more Yoda than God. In any case, this new convention, on the off chance that not heavenly, doesempower confided in joint effort to happen in a world that needs it, and that is apart. Invigorated, we are Over the entire course of time, each new type of media has empowered humankind torise above time, space, and mortality. That — might we venture to say — divine capacitydefinitely brings up over again the existential issue of character: Who are we?What's the significance here to be human? How would we conceptualize ourselves? AsMarshall McLuhan noticed, the medium turns into the message after some time.Individuals shape and are formed by media. Our cerebrums adjust. Our foundationsadjust. Society adjusts."Today you want an association with blessed freedoms to give youwith a personality, similar to a bank card, a regular customer card, or a credit card,"18said Carlos Moreira of WISeKey. Your folks gave you a name, the statelicensed obstetrician or birthing specialist who conveyed you took your impression andvouched for your weight and length, and the two players verified the time,date, and spot of your appearance by marking your introduction to the world declaration. Presently theycan record this declaration on the blockchain and connect birth declarationsfurthermore, a school asset to it. Loved ones can contribute bitcoin to youradvanced education. There, your information stream starts.In the beginning of the Web, Tom Peters expressed, "You are yourprojects."19 He implied that our corporate affiliations and occupation titles no morecharacterized us. What is similarly obvious at this point: "You are your information." Inconvenience is,Moreira said, "That personality is currently yours, yet the information that comes from itsassociation on the planet is claimed by somebody else."20 That is the manner by which mostenterprises and establishments view you, by your information contrail across theWeb. They total your information into a virtual portrayal of you, andthey give this "virtual you" with uncommon new advantages past yourguardians' most joyful dreams.21 Yet comfort accompanies a cost:

protection.The individuals who say "protection is dead — deal with it" are wrong.

Security is theunderpinning of free social orders."Individuals have an exceptionally oversimplified perspective on identity,"23 said blockchainscholar Andreas Antonopoulos. We utilize the word character to portray theself, the projection of that self to the world, and this multitude of qualities that wepartner with that self or one of its projections. These may come fromnature, from the state, from private associations. We might have one ormore jobs and a progression of measurements connected to those jobs, and the jobs maychange. Think about your last work. Did your job change naturally due tochanges in the work that should have been finished or due to updates to yourexpected set of responsibilities?Consider the possibility that "the virtual you" was truth be told possessed by you — your ownsymbol — and "lived" in the black box of your personality so you couldadapt your information stream and uncover just what you expected to, whendeclaring a specific right. For what reason does your driver's permit contain moredata than the way that you have finished your driving assessment andexhibited your capacity to drive? Envision another period of the Web whereyour own symbol oversees and safeguards the items in your black box.This dependable programming worker could deliver just the necessary detail or sumfor every circumstance and simultaneously race up your information morsels as youexplore the computerized world.This might seem like the stuff of sci-fi as depicted in filmslike The Framework or Symbol. In any case, today blockchain advances make itconceivable. Joe Lubin, President of Agreement

Frameworks, alludes to this idea as a"relentless computerized ID and persona" on a blockchain. "I show an alternatepart of myself to my school companions contrasted with when I'm talking atthe Chicago Took care of," he said. "In the web-based computerized economy, I will addressmy different angles and collaborate in that world from the foundation of variouspersonas." Lubin hopes to have a "standard persona," the rendition of himthat covers charges, acquires credits, and gets protection. "I will have maybe abusiness persona and a family persona to isolate the worries that Idecide to connection to my accepted persona. I might have a gamer persona that Itry not to need connected to my business persona. I could try and have a dull webpersona that is never linkable to the others."24Your black box might incorporate data, for example, an officially sanctionedID, Federal retirement aide number, clinical data, administration accounts,monetary records, confirmations, practice licenses, birth declaration, differentdifferent certifications, and data so private you would rather not uncover itbe that as it may, would like to adapt its worth, like sexual inclination or clinicalcondition, for a survey or an exploration study. You could permit these information forexplicit purposes to explicit substances for explicit timeframes. You couldsend a subset of your qualities to your eye specialist and an alternate subset tothe mutual funds that you might want to put resources into. Your symbol could replyindeed no inquiries without uncovering what your identity is: "Are you 21years or more established?

Did you procure more than $100,000 in every one of the last threeyears? Do you have a weight list in the typical range?"25In the actual world, your standing is nearby — your neighborhood businessperson,your manager, your companions at an evening gathering all have a specific assessmentabout you. In the advanced economy, the notorieties of different personas inyour symbol will be versatile. Movability will assist with bringing individuals all over the placeinto the computerized economy. Individuals with a computerized wallet and symbol in Africacould lay out the standing expected to, say, get the means to begin abusiness. "It couldn't be any more obvious, this large number of individuals know me and have vouched for me. I'mmonetarily dependable. I'm an emancipated resident of the worldwide computerizedeconomy."Character is just a little piece of it. The rest is a cloud — a character cloud— of particulates freely or firmly connected to your personality. Assuming we attempt torecord every one of these into the blockchain, a permanent record, we lose not justthe subtlety of social cooperation yet additionally the endowment of neglecting. Individuals shouldnever be characterized by their most awful day.

3. Principles of the Digital Blockchain Coins

Opportunity is predicated on security," said Ann Cavoukian, chiefoverseer of the Security and Huge Information Establishment at Ryerson College. "Ifirst discovered that a long time back when I began going to meetings inGermany. It is no mishap that Germany is the main security and informationassurance country on the planet. They needed to persevere through the maltreatments of the ThirdReich and the total discontinuance of their opportunities as a whole, what beganwith the total evacuation of their protection. At the point when that finished, they said,'Never again."'1Thus it is amusing — or thoroughly fitting — that one of the first decentralizedshared computational stages to ensure client security is calledMystery, additionally the name given to the machine created by German designerArthur Scherbius to translate coded data. Scherbius planned Puzzler for business use: through his gadget, worldwide organizations couldrapidly and securely convey their proprietary innovations, stock tips, and otherinsider data. Inside a couple of years, Germany's tactical powers wereproducing their own variants of Mystery to communicate coded messagesover radio to troops.

During the conflict, the Nazis utilized Conundrum to spreadsmart courses of action, subtleties of targets, and the planning of assaults. It was a device ofenduring and persecution.Our contemporary Conundrum is a device of opportunity and success.Planned at MIT Media Lab by Fellow Zyskind and Oz Nathan, the newConundrum joins the excellencies of blockchain's public record, thestraightforwardness of which "gives solid motivating forces to legit conduct,"with something known as homomorphic encryption and secure multipartycomputation.2 All the more basically, "Riddle takes your data — anydata — splits it up, and scrambles it into bits of information that arehaphazardly circulated to hubs in the organization. There is no such thing as it in one spot,"said Cavoukian. "Mystery utilizes blockchain innovation to insert the informationalso, track every one of the bits of information."3 You can impart it to outsidersfurthermore, those gatherings can involve it in calculations while never decoding it.4 On the off chance that itworks, it could reshape how we approach our own personality on the web. Envisionhaving a black box of your own data that you alone control andcan get to.Regardless of how cool it might sound, there are motivations to carefully stepon the cryptographic boondocks. To start with, it necessities to bootstrap a huge organization ofmembers. Second, "cryptography is a region where you never need to beutilizing the freshest and most noteworthy, on the grounds that there is a whole history of ancalculation that everybody accepts is secure, that is out there for four or fiveyears, and some extremely enlivened researcher will emerge and say, there's an imperfection,furthermore, the whole thing tumbles," said

Austin Slope of Blockstream. "That is the reasonwe by and large lean toward moderate, very deeply grounded, well establishedcalculations.

This stuff is extremely, well future-sealed, and bitcoin wasplanned with that in mind."5In any case, the idea merits treating extremely in a serious way, as it has significantsuggestions for protection, security, and supportability. "Puzzler is advertisingwhat they say ensures security," Cavoukian said. "That is a major case, yetthat is the sort of thing we progressively need in this associated,interconnected world."6In our examination, we ran over various ventures started onblockchain innovations whose designers had comparative desires forempowering essential basic liberties — not just the privileges to protection and security,yet additionally the freedoms to property, acknowledgment as an individual under the law, andcooperation in government, culture, and the economy. Envision ainnovation that could safeguard our opportunity to decide for us as well as ourfamilies, to communicate these decisions on the planet, and to control our ownpredetermination, regardless of where we resided or were conceived. What new devices and newoccupations might we at any point make with those capacities? What new organizations andadministrations? How might we contemplate the valuable open doors? The responses weredirectly before us, praises of Satoshi Nakamoto.

We accept that this next time could be enlivened by Satoshi Nakamoto'svision, planned around a bunch of understood standards, and acknowledged by thecooperative soul of numerous enthusiastic and similarly skilled forerunners in thelocal area.His terrific vision was restricted to cash, not to some more prominent objective ofmaking a second era of the Web. There was no conversation ofreevaluating the firm, changing our foundations, or changing civilizationto improve things. In any case, Satoshi's vision was shocking in its effortlessness,inventiveness, and knowledge into mankind. It turned out to be obvious to the individuals who readthe 2008 paper that another time of the advanced economy was going to start.Where the principal time of the computerized economy was started by an intermingling ofregistering and correspondences advances, this subsequent period would befueled by a sharp mix of PC designing, science,cryptography, and social financial matters.Folksinger Gordon Lightfoot warbled, "In the event that you could guess what I might be thinking,love, everything that a story my contemplations could say." Satoshi has been incommunicadobeginning around 2011 (however the name springs up on conversation loads up from time totime), however we think the trust convention he bootstrapped fitsstandards for reconfiguring our foundations and economy.

Everybody we conversed with has been anxious to share bits of knowledge into blockchaininnovation with us. Every discussion, each white paper, every gathering stringhas surfaced various topics that we've picked apart into planstandards — standards for making programming, administrations, plans of action,markets, associations, and even states on the blockchain. Satoshinever expounded on these standards, yet they are verifiable in the innovationstage he released. We consider them to be standards for molding the following period ofthe advanced economy, and a time of recharged trust.Assuming you're new to this space, we trust these standards will help youcomprehend the nuts and bolts of the blockchain unrest. On the off chance that you're a die-harddoubter of the bitcoin blockchain, they ought to in any case serve you as youconsider your future as a business visionary, innovator, specialist, or craftsman wholooks for inventive joint efforts with similar individuals; as a proprietor orfinancial backer in resources of various types; or as a chief who needs to reconsider yourjob in this beginning blockchain economy. 1. Organized HonestyStandard: Trust is natural, not outward. Respectability is encoded in each stepof the cycle and appropriated, not vested in any single part. Memberscan trade esteem straightforwardly with the assumption that the other party willHonorable act. That implies that the upsides of trustworthiness — genuineness in one'swords and deeds, thought for others' inclinations, responsibility for theresults of one's choices and activities, and straightforwardness in choicemaking and move making — are coded in choice privileges, motivating forcedesigns, and activities so that acting without uprightness either isinconceivable or costs much additional time, cash, energy, and notoriety.Issue to Be Settled: On the Web, individuals haven't had the option toexecute or carry on with work straightforwardly for the basic explanation that cash isn't likeother data products and licensed innovation fundamentally. You can send thesame selfie to every one of your companions, yet you should not give your companion a dollarthat you've proactively given to another person.

The cash should leave youraccount and go into your companion's. It can't exist in the two spots, not to mentiondifferent spots. As there's a gamble of your spending a unit of computerizedmoney in two places and having one of them skip like a terrible check.That is known as the twofold spend issue. That is great for fraudsters whoneed to spend their cash two times. It's terrible for the beneficiary of the skippedsum and terrible for your standing on the web. Generally, while makingonline installments, we tackle the twofold spend issue by clearing eachexchange through the focal information bases of one or many outsiders, suchas a cash move administration (like Western Association), a business bank(Citicorp), an administration body (District Bank of Australia), a creditcard organization (Visa), or a web-based installment stage (PayPal). Settlementcan require days or even a long time in certain regions of the planet.Forward leap: Satoshi utilized a current dispersed distributednetwork and a touch of shrewd cryptography to make an agreement systemthat could tackle the twofold spend issue as well as, while possibly worse than, aconfided in outsider. On the bitcoin blockchain, the organization time-stamps thefirst exchange where the proprietor spends a specific coin and rejectsresulting spends of the coin, subsequently dispensing with a twofold spend. Networkmembers who run completely working bitcoin hubs — called diggers — accumulateup late exchanges, settle them as a block of information, and rehashthe cycle like clockwork. Each block should allude to the previous blockto be substantial. The conventions likewise incorporate a technique for recovering circle spacewith the goal that all hubs can proficiently store the full blockchain. At long last, theblockchain is public. Anybody can see exchanges occurring. Nobody canconceal an exchange, and that makes bitcoin more discernible than cash.Satoshi looked for not exclusively to disintermediate the focal financial powersyet in addition to take out the equivocalness and clashing understandings of whatoccurred. Allow the code to justify itself. Allow the organization to arrive at agreementalgorithmically on what occurred and record it cryptographically on theblockchain. The component for arriving at agreement is basic. "Agreementis a social interaction," published content to a blog Vitalik Buterin, trailblazer of the Ethereumblockchain. "People are genuinely great at participating in agreement . . .with next to no assistance from calculations." He made sense of that, when a framework scalespast a singular's capacity to figure it out, individuals go to programmingspecialists. In distributed networks, the agreement calculation evenly divides theright to refresh the situation with the organization, that is to say, to decide on reality. Thecalculation gives out this right to a gathering of friends who comprise anfinancial set, a set that has a dog in the fight, in a manner of speaking. As perButerin, what's significant about this financial set is that its individuals aresafely disseminated: no single part or cartel ought to have the option to overwhelma larger part, regardless of whether they had the means and motivator to do so.7To accomplish agreement, the bitcoin network utilizes what's known as a proof ofwork (PoW) component. This might sound muddled yet the thought is abasic one. Since we can't depend on the character of the excavators to choosewho makes the following block, we rather make a riddle that is difficult to settle(i.e., it takes a ton of work), yet simple to confirm (i.e., every other person can checkthe response rapidly). Members concur that whoever tackles theissue initially will make the following block. Excavators need to consume assets(registering equipment and power) to settle the riddle by seeing as theright hash, a sort of novel unique mark for a text or an information document. For eachblock they find, excavators get bitcoin as a prize. The riddle isnumerically put in a position to make it difficult to track down an easy route to settle it.That is the reason, when the remainder of the organization sees the response, everybody truststhat a ton of work went into creating it. Likewise, this puzzle settling isconsistent "to the tune of 500,000 trillion hashes each second," as indicated byDino Imprint Angaritis. Excavators are "searching for a hash that meets the objective.Happening like clockwork is genuinely bound. It's a Poisson interaction, sothat occasionally it requires one moment and now and again 60 minutes, yet by and large,it's ten minutes."

Angaritis made sense of how it functions: "Diggers assemble all theforthcoming exchanges that they track down on the organization and run the information througha cryptographic summary capability called the safe hash calculation (SHA256), which yields a 32-byte hash esteem. In the event that the hash esteem is under acertain objective (set by the organization and changed each 2,016 blocks), then, at that point, thedigger has tracked down the response to the riddle and has 'tackled' the block.Tragically for the digger, it is truly challenging to track down the right hash esteem. Ifthe hash esteem is off-base, the excavator changes the information marginally and attemptsonce more. Each endeavor brings about a completely unique hash esteem. Diggers haveto attempt ordinarily to track down the right response. As of November 2015, thenumber of hash endeavors is on normal 350 million trillion. That is a great deal of work!"8You might catch wind of other agreement systems. The principal rendition of the Ethereum blockchain — Wilderness — additionally utilizes verification of work, yet entirely thedesigners of Ethereum 1.1 hope to supplant it with a proof of stakesystem. Confirmation of stake expects diggers to put resources into and cling to somestore of significant worth (i.e., the local badge of the blockchain like Peercoin,NXT, and so on.).

They shouldn't for a second need to burn through effort to cast a ballot. Other blockchains, for example,Swell and Heavenly, depend on informal organizations for agreement and maysuggest that new members (i.e., new hubs) create a remarkable hubrundown of no less than 100 hubs they can confide in deciding on the condition ofissues. This sort of verification is one-sided: newbies need social insight andnotoriety to partake. Confirmation of movement is another component; itjoins confirmation of work and evidence of stake, where an irregular number ofdiggers should approve the block utilizing a cryptokey before the blockbecomes official.9 Verification of limit expects diggers to dispense a sizablevolume of their hard drive to mining. A comparable idea, confirmation of capacity,expects excavators to dispense and share circle space in a circulated cloud.Capacity matters. Information on blockchains are not quite the same as information on theWeb in one significant manner. On the Web, the vast majority of the data ispliable and short lived, and the specific date and season of its distribution isn'tbasic to past or future data. On the blockchain, bitcoin developmentacross the organization is forever stam Subsequently, the blockchain should besaved completely.So significant are the cycles of mining — collecting a block ofexchanges, going through some asset, tackling the issue, coming toagreement, keeping a duplicate of the full record — that some have called thebitcoin blockchain a public utility like the Web, a utility that requirespublic help.

Paul Brody of Ernst and Youthful thinks that every one of our machinesought to give their handling capacity to the upkeep of a blockchain: "Yourlawnmower or dishwasher will accompany a central processor that is most likely amultiple times more remarkable than it very, thus why not have itmine? Not to make you cash, but rather to keep up with your portionof the blockchain,"10 he said. No matter what the agreement system, theblockchain guarantees respectability through cunning code instead of through humancreatures who decide to make the best decision.Suggestions for the Blockchain Economy: As opposed to trusting enormousorganizations and legislatures to confirm individuals' personalities and vouch for theirnotorieties, we can trust the organization. Unexpectedly, we have astage that guarantees trust in exchanges and much recorded dataregardless of how the other party acts.The ramifications for generally friendly, political, and financial movement arefaltering. It's not just about who wedded whom, who decided in favor of whom,who paid whom, about any undertaking requires confided in records andguaranteed exchanges. Who claims what? Who holds which freedoms to thisprotected innovation? Who moved on from clinical school? Who purchasedweapons? Who made these Nike shoes, this Apple gadget, or this child recipe?Where did these jewels come from? Trust is the sine qua non of thecomputerized economy, and a stage for secure and solid mass coordinated effortholds numerous opportunities for another sort of association and society.2. Circulated PowerStandard: The framework disseminates power across a distributed organization withno single place of control. No single party can close the framework down. If afocal authority figures out how to pass out or remove an individual or gathering, theframework will in any case get by. On the off chance that over around 50% of the organization endeavors to overpower theentire, everybody will see what's going on.Issue to Be Settled: In the principal period of the Web, any hugeorganization with a huge laid out base of clients, be they representatives,residents, clients, or different associations, barely cared about their socialcontract.

Endlessly time once more, focal powers have demonstrated that they'rewilling and ready to abrogate clients, distribution center and dissect client information,answer government demands for information without clients' information, andcarry out enormous scope changes without clients' assent.Leap forward: The energy expenses of overwhelming the bitcoinblockchain would offset the monetary advantages. Satoshi conveyed aconfirmation of-work strategy that expects clients to exhaust a great deal of figuringpower (which requires a ton of power) to safeguard the organization and mintnew coins. He was enlivened by cryptographer Adam Back's answer,Hashcash, to relieve spam and disavowal of-administration assaults. Back's strategyexpected e-mailers to give confirmation of work while sending the message. It inimpact stepped "unique conveyance" on an email to flag the message'ssignificance to its shipper. "This message is basic to such an extent that I've burned through thisenergy in sending it to you." It builds the expenses of sending spam,malware, and ransomware.Anybody can download the bitcoin convention free of charge and keep a duplicateof the blockchain. It influences bootstrapping, a method for transferring theprogram onto a worker's PC or cell phone through a couplestraightforward directions that put the remainder of the program into high gear. It's completelycirculated across a worker network like BitTorrent, a common data set oflicensed innovation that lives on huge number of PCsaround the world.Undoubtedly, this safeguards the organization from the hands of the state, whichcould be positive or negative contingent upon the circumstance — say a nonconformist in aextremist nation battling for ladies' privileges versus a criminal in avote based country directing coercion. Extremist systems proved unablefreeze ledgers or hold onto assets of political activists. States proved unablerandomly hold onto resources on the blockchain as Franklin Delano Roosevelt'sorganization did through FDR's Leader Request 6102, which requiredresidents to turn their "gold coin, gold bullion, and gold endorsements" over tothe public authority or hazard fines or imprisonment.11 Josh Fairfield ofWashington and Lee College put it gruffly: "There's no mediator to goafter anymore."12 The blockchain lives all over. Volunteers keep up withit by keeping their duplicate of the blockchain state-of-the-art and loaning their extraPC handling units for mining. No indirect access managing. Each activityor on the other hand exchange is communicated across the organization for ensuing confirmationfurthermore, approval. Nothing goes through a focal outsider; nothing isput away on a focal server.Satoshi likewise circulated the mint by connecting the issuance of bitcoins tothe production of another block in the record, putting the ability to mint into allthe hands of the friend organization. Whichever excavator tackled the riddle andsubmitted evidence of work initially could get various new bitcoins. Thereis no Central bank, national bank, or depository with command over the cashsupply. In addition, each bitcoin contains direct connections to its beginning block andevery ensuing exchange.So no mediators are required. The working of the blockchain ismass coordinated effort at its ideal. You have control over your information, yourproperty, and your degree of cooperation. It's conveyed figuring powerempowering appropriated and aggregate human power.Suggestions for the Blockchain Economy: Maybe such a stagecould empower new dispersed models of abundance creation. Maybe new sortsof distributed joint efforts could focus on mankind's generally vexing socialissues. Maybe we could tackle the emergency of certainty and evenauthenticity in the present establishments by moving genuine power toward residents,furnishing them with genuine open doors for success and support insociety, as opposed to through PR craftiness.3. Esteem as Motivating forceRule: The framework adjusts the motivating forces, everything being equal. Bitcoin orsome badge of significant worth is basic to this arrangement and corresponding ofnotoriety. Satoshi modified the product to remunerate the individuals who work onit and have a place with the people who hold and utilize its tokens, so they all fare thee wellof it. Kind of a definitive Tamagotchi, the blockchain is an internationallycirculated home egg.13Issue to Be

Addressed: In the primary time of the Web, the focusof force in organizations, joined with their sheer size, intricacy, andhaziness, empowered them to remove lopsided worth from the verynetworks that blessed them with freedoms. Huge banks took advantage of themonetary framework to its limit since "motivation structures by and largeof the top chiefs and a large number of the loaning officials of these banks [were]intended to support limited conduct and exorbitant gamble taking,"as indicated by business analyst Joseph Stiglitz. That included "going after theleast fortunate Americans."

He summarized the issue: "On the off chance that you give individuals awfulimpetuses, they act severely, and they acted similarly as one would haveexpected."14Huge dab coms hung free administrations in retail, search, and virtual entertainmentin return for client information. As per an Ernst and Youthful review, almost66% of supervisors surveyed said they gathered buyer information to drivebusiness, and almost 80% professed to have expanded incomes fromthis information mining. In any case, when these organizations get hacked, it's the purchasers whoneed to tidy up the wreck of taken Mastercard and ledgerdata. It's not shocking that, in a similar overview, almost 50% ofshoppers said they'd be removing admittance to their information in the following fiveyears, and over half said they were at that point giving less information, includingcontrolling themselves via virtual entertainment, than in the past five years.15Leap forward: Satoshi anticipated that members should act in their own selfinterests. He figured out game hypothesis. He knew that organizations withoutguardians have been defenseless against Sybil assaults, where hubs fashionvarious personalities, weaken freedoms, and devalue the worth of reputation.16The uprightness of the shared organization and the standing of its friends bothdecrease on the off chance that you don't realize whether you're managing three gatherings or oneparty utilizing three characters. So Satoshi customized the source code so that,regardless of how childishly individuals acted, their activities would help the frameworkgenerally speaking and build to their notorieties, but they decided to distinguishthemselves.

The asset necessities of the agreement component,joined with bitcoins as remuneration, could force members to do the rightthing, seeming to be OK that they were unsurprising.Sybil assaults would be monetarily unviable.Satoshi stated, "By show, the principal exchange in a block is aunique exchange that begins another coin possessed by the maker of the block.This adds a motivator for hubs to help the network."17 Bitcoin is animpetus for diggers to take part in making a block and connecting it to thepast block. The individuals who complete a block initially get an amount of bitcoinsfor their endeavors. Satoshi's convention compensated early adopters abundantlywith bitcoin: for the initial four years, diggers got 50 bitcoins (BTC) foreach block. At regular intervals, the prize per block would split: 25 BTC,12.5 BTC, etc. Since they currently own bitcoin, they have a motivatorto guarantee the stage's drawn out progress, purchasing the best hardware torun mining tasks, burning through effort as proficiently as could be expected, andkeeping up with the record. Bitcoin is likewise a case on throughproprietorship in the actual stage. Dispersed client accounts are the mostfundamental component of the cryptographic organization framework. By buying andutilizing bitcoin, one is supporting the blockchain's turn of events.Satoshi picked as the monetary set the proprietors of registering power. Thisrequires these diggers to consume an asset outer to the organization,to be specific power, to partake in the prize framework. Each sofrequently, various diggers find two similarly substantial blocks of equivalent level, and therest of the excavators should pick which block to expand on straightaway. They for the most partpick whichever they think will win instead of expanding on both, on the grounds thatthey'd in any case need to part their handling power between the forks, andthat is a methodology for losing esteem. The longest chain addresses the bestmeasure of work and hence members pick it as the sanctioned condition ofthe blockchain. Interestingly, Ethereum picked proprietors of coin as its monetaryset. Swell and Heavenly picked the informal organization.The Catch 22 of these agreement plans is that by acting in one's selfinterest, one is serving the shared (P2P) organization, and that thuslyinfluences one's standing as an individual from the financial set. Before blockchainadvances, individuals couldn't without much of a stretch influence the worth of their standingon the web. It wasn't simply because of Sybil assaults, where a PC couldpossess various jobs.

Character is complex, nuanced, and transient. Fewindividuals see all sides, not to mention the nuances and the bend of our personality. Forvarious settings, we need to create some report or other to verifysome detail of our personality. Individuals "without papers" are restricted toworking together with their group of friends. On blockchains like Heavenly, that is anfantastic beginning, a method for making a tenacious computerized presence andlaying out standing that is versatile well past one's geographiclocal area.One more leap forward to save esteem is the money related arrangementmodified into the product. "All cash humankind has at any point utilized has beenuncertain somehow," said Scratch Szabo. "This weakness has beenappeared in a wide assortment of ways, from forging to robbery, yet all at once thegenerally noxious of which has presumably been inflation."18 Satoshi covered thesupply of bitcoins at 21 million to be given after some time to forestall erraticexpansion. Provided the dividing with like clockwork of bitcoins mined in a blockalso, the ongoing pace of mining — six blocks each hour — those 21 million BTCought to be available for use around the year 2140. No excessive inflation ormoney degrading brought about by clumsy or degenerate administrations.Monetary forms are not by any means the only resources that we can exchange on the blockchain."We've simply started to start to expose what's underneath on what's conceivable," expressed Slope ofBlockstream. "We're currently at that 1994 point with regards to applications andconventions that truly exploit the organization and show the world,'This is the very thing that you can do that is absolutely groundbreaking.'"19 Slope hopes tosee different monetary instruments, from proof-of-resource legitimacy toevidence of-property proprietorship. He additionally hopes to see bitcoin applications inthe Metaverse (a virtual reality) where you can change over bitcoin intoKongbucks and enlist Hiro Hero to hack you some data.20 Or jackyourself into the Desert garden (a universe of various virtual utopias) where youin reality in all actuality do find the Hidden little goody, win Halliday's bequest, permit Desert garden'svirtual situating freedoms to research, and purchase a self-driving vehicle to exploreToronto.21What's more, obviously, there's the Web of Things, where we register ourgadgets, allot them a personality (Intel is as of now doing this), and directioninstallment among them utilizing bitcoin instead of various government issued types of money."You can characterize every one of these new business cases that you need to do, and haveit interoperate inside the organization, and utilize the organization foundationwithout bootstrapping a new blockchain, only for yourself," said Slope.22Dissimilar to government issued money, each bitcoin is distinct to eight decimal spots. Itempowers clients to join and part esteem over the long run in a solitary exchange,implying that an info can have various results over numerous times oftime, which is definitely more proficient than a progression of exchanges. Clients can setup brilliant agreements to meter utilization of a help and make little parts ofinstallments at customary stretches.Suggestions for the Blockchain Economy: The main time of theWeb missed this. Presently we have a stage where individuals and eventhings have legitimate monetary motivators to team up actually and makepretty much anything. Envision online conversation bunches where membershave notorieties worth improving, to some degree since awful conduct will costthem monetarily. Savages need not make a difference. Envision a shared organization ofsunlight based chargers where mortgage holders get continuous pay on theblockchain for creating manageable energy. Envision an open sourceprogramming project where a local area of designers redressessupercontributors for satisfactory code. Envision there's no nations. It isn'thard to do.234. SecurityGuideline: Wellbeing measures are implanted in the organization with no singleweak spot, and they give privacy, yet in additionvalidness and nonrepudiation to activity of any kind. Anybody who needs totake an interest should utilize cryptography — quitting isn't a choice — and theresults of crazy way of behaving are segregated to the individual who actedwildly.Issue to Be Addressed: Hacking, wholesale fraud, misrepresentation, cyberbullying,phishing, spam, malware, ransomware — these sabotage the securityof the person in the public eye. The principal time of the Web, instead of bringingstraightforwardness and weakening infringement, appears to have done essentially nothing to incrementsecurity of people, establishments, and financial movement. The normalWeb client frequently needs to depend on feeble passwords to safeguard email andonline records since specialist co-ops or businesses don't demand anythingmore grounded. Think about the regular monetary delegate: it doesn't represent considerable authority increating secure innovation; it has practical experience in monetary advancement. In theyear that Satoshi distributed his white paper, information breaks at such monetaryfirms as BNY Mellon, Countrywide, and GE Cash represented north of 50percent of all personality robberies detailed that year, as per the CharacterBurglary Asset Center.24 By 2014, that figure had tumbled to 5.5 percent forthe monetary area, yet penetrates in clinical and medical care leaped to 42percent of the year's aggregate.

IBM revealed that the normal expense of an informationbreak is $3.8 million, and that implies that information breaks have cost in any event$1.5 billion over the last two years.25 The typical expense for a person ofclinical personality misrepresentation is near $13,500, and offenses are on the ascent.Customers don't know which part of their life will be hacked next.26 Ifthe following phase of the advanced upheaval includes imparting cashstraightforwardly between parties, then, at that point, correspondence should be hackproof.Leap forward: Satoshi expected members to utilize public keyframework (PKI) for laying out a protected stage. PKI is a high leveltype of "hilter kilter" cryptography, where clients get two keys that don'tcarry out a similar role: one is for encryption and one for unscrambling.Consequently, they are deviated. The bitcoin blockchain is currently the biggestregular citizen organization of PKI on the planet, and second generally to the U.S.Branch of Protection normal access system.27Spearheaded in the 1970s,28 hilter kilter cryptography acquired somefooting during the 1990s as email encryption freeware, for example,Very Great Protection. PGP is really secure, and basically a problem to utilizesince everybody in your organization should utilize it, and you need tomonitor your two keys and everybody's public keys. There's nosecret key reset capability. In the event that you fail to remember yours, you need to start from the very beginning.As per the Virtru Organization, "the utilization of email encryption is on therise.

All things considered, just 50% of messages are scrambled on the way, and start to finishemail encryption is more uncommon still."29 Certain individuals utilize advanced authentications,bits of code that safeguard messages without the scramble decodeactivities, however clients should apply (and pay a yearly charge) for their personauthentications, and the most well-known email administrations — Google, Viewpoint, andHurray! — don't uphold them."Past plans fizzled in light of the fact that they needed motivation, and individuals nevervalued protection as motivating force to the point of getting those systems,"30Andreas Antonopoulos said. The bitcoin blockchain settles essentially every one of theseissues by giving the impetus to wide reception of PKI for allexchanges of significant worth, using bitcoin as well as in theshared bitcoin conventions. We shouldn't even bother with frail firewalls, stealingrepresentatives, or protection programmers. On the off chance that we're both utilizing bitcoin, in the event that we can storewhat's more, trade bitcoin safely, then, at that point, we can store and trade exceptionallysecret data and computerized resources safely on the blockchain.This is the secret. Computerized money isn't put away in a record fundamentally. It'saddressed by exchanges showed by a cryptographic hash. Clients holdthe cryptokeys to their own cash and execute straightforwardly with each other.With this security comes the obligation of keeping one's hidden keysprivate.Security principles matter.

The bitcoin blockchain runs on the very wellknown and laid out SHA-256 distributed by the U.S. Public Foundation ofPrinciples and Innovation and acknowledged as a U.S. Government DataHandling Standard. The trouble of the numerous redundancies of thisnumerical estimation expected to find a block arrangement powers thecomputational gadget to consume significant power to settle apuzzle and procure new bitcoin. Different calculations, for example, evidence of stake consumesubstantially less energy.

4. Discovery of the Digital Currency

The worldwide monetary framework moves trillions of dollars everyday, servesbillions of individuals, and supports a worldwide economy worth more than$100 trillion.1 It's the world's most impressive industry, the groundwork ofworldwide free enterprise, and its chiefs are known as the Experts of the Universe.Closer up, it's a Rube Goldberg contraption of lopsided turns of events anddodd inconsistencies. To start with, the machine hasn't had a redesign in some time.New innovation has been welded onto maturing foundation haphazard.Consider the bank offering Web banking yet at the same time giving paper checksalso, running centralized server PCs from the 1970s. At the point when one of itsclients taps her Mastercard on a cutting edge card peruser to purchase aStarbucks grande latte, her cash goes through no less than fivevarious go-betweens prior to arriving at Starbucks' financial balance.

Theexchange requires seconds to clear yet days to settle.Then, at that point, there are the huge multinationals like Apple or GE that need tokeep many financial balances in nearby monetary forms all over the planetjust to work with their operations.2 At the point when such a company needs to movecash between two auxiliaries in two distinct nations, the administrator ofone auxiliary sends a bank wire from his activity's financial balance to theother

47

auxiliary's financial balance. These exchanges are unnecessarily confoundedalso, require days, some of the time a long time to settle. During that time, not one or the otherauxiliary can utilize the cash to subsidize activities or speculation, yet all the same thego-betweens can acquire interest on the float. "The appearance of innovationbasically took paper-based processes and transformed them into semiautomated,semielectronic processes yet the rationale was still paper based," said VikramPandit, previous Chief of Citigroup.3Everywhere, another strange oddity: Dealers tradeprotections on the world's stock trades in nanoseconds; their exchanges clearright away however require three entire days to settle. Nearby states utilize no lessthan ten distinct specialists — guides, legal advisors, back up plans, financiers, and the sky is the limit from there —to work with the issuance of a civil bond.4 A day worker in LosAngeles changes out his check at a cash store for a 4 percent expense, and afterwardstrolls his fistful of dollars over to a corner shop to wire it home to hisfamily in Guatemala, where he gets dinged again on level charges, traderates, and other secret expenses. When his family has evenly divided the totalamong its numerous individuals, no one has to the point of opening a financial balance orget credit. They are among the 2.2 billion individuals who live on under twodollars daily.5 The installments they need to make are little, excessively little forregular installment organizations, for example, charge and Mastercards, whereleast expenses make alleged micropayments incomprehensible.

THE Brilliant EIGHT: HOW THE Monetary AdministrationsArea WILL CHANGEHere are what we accept to be the eight center capabilities ready for disturbance.They are likewise summed up in the table here.1. Validating Personality and Worth: Today we depend on strongmediators to lay out trust and check personality in a monetaryexchange. These middle people are a definitive mediators for accessto fundamental monetary administrations, for example, ledgers and advances.Blockchain brings down and here and there takes out trust by and large incertain exchanges. The innovation will likewise empower companions tolay out personality that is certain, vigorous, and cryptographicallysecure and to lay out trust when trust is required.2.

Moving Worth: Day to day, the monetary framework moves cash aroundthe world, ensuring that no dollar is spent two times: from the99 penny acquisition of a melody on iTunes to the exchange ofbillions of dollars to settle an intracompany store move, buya resource, or gain an organization. Blockchain can turn into thenormal norm for the development of anything of significant worth — monetary standards, stocks, bonds, and titles — in bunches of all shapes and sizes, todistances all over, and to counterparties known and obscure.Subsequently, blockchain can accomplish for the development of significant worth what thestandard steel trailer accomplished for the development of products:decisively lower cost, further develop speed, lessen grating, and liftfinancial development and flourishing.3. Putting away Worth: Monetary organizations are the storehouses of significant worthfor individuals, foundations, and legislatures. For the regular person, abank stores esteem in a wellbeing store box, a bank account, or afinancial records. For enormous establishments that need prepared liquiditywith the assurance of a little profit from their money counterparts, socalled sans risk speculations, for example, currency market reserves orDepository bills will get the job done. People need not depend on banksas the essential stores of significant worth or as suppliers of reserve funds andfinancial records, and establishments will have a more effectivecomponent to purchase and hold sans risk monetary resources.4. Loaning Worth: From family home loans to T-bills, monetaryorganizations work with the issuance of acknowledge, for example, Mastercard obligation,contracts, corporate securities, civil securities, government securities,furthermore, resource supported protections. The loaning business has produced anumber of auxiliary businesses that perform credit checks, creditscores, and credit scores. For the individual, it's a FICO rating. Fora foundation, it's a credit score — from speculation grade to garbage.On the blockchain, anybody will actually want to issue, exchange, and settleconventional obligation instruments straightforwardly, consequently lessening erosion andrisk by speeding up and straightforwardness. Buyers will be capableto get to credits from peers. This is especially critical for theworld's unbanked and for business visionaries all over.5.

Trading Worth: Day to day, showcases worldwide work with thetrade of trillions of dollars of monetary resources. Exchanging is thetrading of resources and monetary instruments for themotivation behind money management, conjecturing, supporting, and arbitraging andincorporates the posttrade life pattern of clearing, settling, and putting awayesteem. Blockchain cuts settlement times on all exchanges fromlong stretches of time to minutes and seconds. This speed and productivitysets out open doors for unbanked and underbanked individuals totake part in abundance creation.6. Subsidizing and Money management: Putting resources into a resource, organization, or newendeavor offers an individual the chance to procure a return, in thetype of capital appreciation, profits, interest, rents, or somemix. The business makes markets: coordinating financial backers withbusiness people and entrepreneurs at each phase of development — fromholy messengers to Initial public offerings and then some. Fund-raising typically requiresmediators — speculation investors, financial speculators, andlegal counselors to give some examples. The blockchain computerizes a significant number of thesecapabilities, empowers new models for shared supporting, and couldadditionally make recording profits and paying coupons more productive,straightforward, and secure.7. Guaranteeing Worth and Overseeing Hazard: Chance administration, ofwhich protection is a subset, is expected to safeguard people andorganizations from questionable misfortune or calamity. All the more extensively, riskthe board in monetary business sectors has generated horde subsidiaryitems and other monetary instruments intended to fence againstcapricious or wild occasions. Last time anyone checked the notionalworth of all remarkable over-the-counter subordinates is $600trillion.

Blockchain upholds decentralized models for protection,utilizing subordinates for risk the executives undeniably morestraightforward. Utilizing reputational frameworks in view of an individual's socialfurthermore, monetary capital, their activities, and other reputationalcredits, guarantors will have a much more clear picture of the actuarialrisk and can pursue more educated choices.8. Representing Worth: Bookkeeping is the estimation,handling, and correspondence of monetary data aboutmonetary substances. It is a multibillion-dollar industry constrained byfour gigantic review firms — Deloitte Well played Tohmatsu,PricewaterhouseCoopers, Ernst and Youthful, and KPMG. Customarybookkeeping practices won't endure the speed and intricacy ofpresent day finance. New bookkeeping techniques utilizing blockchain'sdispersed record will make review and monetary announcingstraightforward and happen continuously. It will likewise emphatically move alongthe limit with regards to controllers and different partners to investigatemonetary activities inside a partnership.

Banks essentiallytry not to see serving these individuals as a "productive recommendation," as indicated by aongoing Harvard Business college study.6 Thus the cash machine isn'treally worldwide in scale and extension.Money related strategy creators and monetary controllers frequently get themselvescoming up short on the real factors, on account of the arranged murkiness of numerous enormous monetarytasks and the compartmentalization of oversight. The worldwide monetaryemergency of 2008 was a valid example. Overabundance influence, an absence of straightforwardness,what's more, a feeling of carelessness driven by slanted motivators forestalled anybodyfrom recognizing the issue until it was almost past the point of no return. "How could youhave anything work, from the police power to a financial framework, if youtry not to have numbers and areas?" contemplated Hernando de Soto.7Controllers are as yet attempting to deal with this machine with rules contrived for themodern age. In New

York State, cash transmission regulations date back to theNationwide conflict when the essential method for moving cash around was horse andbuggy.It's Franken-finance, brimming with crazy inconsistencies, confusions, hotlines, and strain pots. Why, for instance, does Western Association need500,000 retail locations all over the planet, when the greater part the world'spopulace has a brilliant phone?8 Erik Voorhees, an early bitcoin pioneer andfrank pundit of the financial framework, told us, "Mailing an anvil is quickerto China than it is to send cash through the financial framework to China.That is insane! Cash is now advanced, dislike they're transporting bedsof money when you do a wire!"

For what reason is it so wasteful? As per Paul David, the financial expert whobegat the term efficiency Catch 22, laying new innovations over existingframework is "entirely normal during authentic changes from onemechanical worldview to the next."10 For instance, producers requiredforty years to embrace business jolt over steam power, andfrequently the two worked one next to the other before makers at last exchangedover for good. During that time of retrofitting, efficiency as a matter of factdiminished. In the monetary framework, in any case, the issue is compoundedsince there has been no perfect change starting with one innovation then onto the next;there are various inheritance advances, approximately many years old, neververy satisfying their maximum capacity.Why? To some extent, since finance is a syndication business.

In his evaluation of the monetary emergency, Nobel laureate Joseph Stiglitz composed thatbanks "were doing all that they could to increment exchange costs inall ways imaginable." That's what he contended, even at the retail level, installments foressential labor and products "ought to cost a negligible portion of a penny." "Yet howmuch do they charge?" he pondered. "One, two, or three percent of theworth of what is sold or more. Capital and sheer scale, joined with aadministrative and social permit to work permits banks to extricate as much asthey can, in a large number of nations, particularly in the US, makingbillions of dollars of profits."11 All things considered, the chance for hugeunified mediators has been colossal. Not just conventional banks(e.g., Bank of America), yet additionally charge card organizations (Visa), venturebanks (Goldman Sachs), stock trades (NYSE), clearinghouses (CME),wire/settlement administrations (Western Association), guarantors (Lloyd's), protections regulationfirms (Skadden, Arps), national banks (Central bank), resourcesupervisors (BlackRock), accountancies (Deloitte), consultancies(Accenture), and products dealers (Vitol Gathering) make up this far reachingleviathan. The cog wheels of the monetary framework — strong go-betweens thatsolidify capital and impact and frequently force imposing business model financial matters —make the framework work, yet additionally dial it back, add cost, and produceoutsized advantages for themselves. Due to their imposing business model position, numerousoccupants have no impetus to further develop items, increment productivity,further develop the purchaser experience, or appeal to the future.Office holders have no impetus to further develop items, increment effectiveness,further develop the buyer experience, or appeal to the future.The times of Franken-finance are numbered as blockchain innovationvows to make the following ten years one of incredible disturbance and disengagement yetadditionally monstrous chance for the people who hold onto it.

The worldwide monetaryadministrations industry today is loaded with issues: It is outdated, based onmany years old innovation that is in conflict with our quickly progressing computerizedworld, making it regularly sluggish and untrustworthy. It is selective, leavingbillions of individuals with no admittance to essential monetary devices. It is concentrated,presenting it to information breaks, different assaults, or out and out disappointment. What's more, it ismonopolistic, supporting business as usual and smothering advancement. Blockchainvows to tackle these issues and a lot more as pioneers andbusiness visionaries devise better approaches to make esteem on this strong stage.There are six key motivations behind why blockchain innovation will achievesignificant changes to this industry, busting the money syndication, andoffering people and establishments the same genuine decision by they way they make andoversee esteem. Industry members the world over ought to pay heed.Validation: Without precedent for history, two gatherings who not one or the otherknow nor trust each other can execute and carry on with work. Checkingcharacter and laying out trust is as of now not the right and honor ofthe monetary mediator. Additionally, with regards to monetaryadministrations, the trust convention takes on a two sided connotation.

Theblockchain can likewise lay out trust when trust is required by confirmingthe personality and limit of any counterparty through a mixof past exchange history (on the blockchain), notoriety scoresin light of total audits, and other social and financialmarkers.Cost: On the blockchain, the organization the two clears and settles peerto-peer esteem moves, and it does so ceaselessly so that its recordis dependably cutting-edge. First off, assuming banks bridled that ability,they could dispense with an expected $20 billion in administrative centercosts without changing their fundamental plan of action,as per the Spanish bank Santander, however the genuine numberis without a doubt a lot more noteworthy.12 With drastically lower costs, banks couldoffer people and organizations more noteworthy admittance to monetary administrations,markets, and capital in underserved networks. This can be ahelp not exclusively to officeholders yet additionally to sketchy upstarts andbusiness visionaries all over. Anybody, anyplace, with a PDAfurthermore, a Web association could take advantage of the huge corridors of worldwidefinance.Speed: Today, settlements require three to seven days to settle. Stockexchanges require a few days, though bank credit exchanges take onnormal a stunning 23 days to settle.13 The Quicknetwork handles fifteen million installment arranges a day between tenthousand monetary establishments around the world yet requires days to clear andsettle them.14 The equivalent is valid for the Robotized Clearing House(ACH) framework, which handles trillions of dollars of U.S. installmentsevery year. The bitcoin network takes a normal of ten minutes toclear and settle all exchanges led during that period.

Otherblockchain networks are considerably quicker, and new developments, for example,the Bitcoin Lightning Organization, intend to emphatically scale thelimit of the bitcoin blockchain while dropping settlement andgetting times to a portion free from a second.15 "In the comparingbanking world, where you have a source in one organization and acollector in another, you need to go through different records,various delegates, different jumps. Things can in a real sense flop inthe center. There's a wide range of capital prerequisites for that," saidSwell Labs President Chris Larsen.16 Without a doubt, the shift to moment andfrictionless worth exchange would let loose capital in any case caught intravel, awful news for anybody benefitting from the float.Risk The board: Blockchain innovation vows to moderatea few types of monetary gamble. The first is settlement risk, the gamblethat your exchange will return in view of some error in thesettlement process. The second is counterparty risk, the gamble thatyour counterparty will default prior to settling an exchange. The mosthuge is fundamental gamble, the all out amount of all remarkablecounterparty risk in the framework. Vikram Pandit called this Herstattrisk, named after a German bank that couldn't meet its liabilitiesalso, hence went under: "We viewed as through the monetaryemergency one of the dangers was, in the event that I'm exchanging with someone, how would Irealize they will choose the opposite side?" As perPandit, moment settlement on the blockchain could wipe out thatrisk totally. Bookkeepers could investigate the inward functions ofan organization anytime and see which exchanges werehappening and how the organization was recording them. Unalterable qualityof an exchange and moment compromise of monetary detailingwould dispense with one part of organization risk — the gamble thatcorrupt chiefs will take advantage of the lumbering documentation andhuge time postponement to disguise bad behavior.

Esteem Advancement: The bitcoin blockchain was intended formoving bitcoins, not so much for taking care of other monetary resources. Notwithstanding,the innovation is open source, welcoming trial and error. Sometrailblazers are creating separate blockchains, known as altcoins,worked for some different option from bitcoin installments. Others are lookingto use the bitcoin blockchain's size and liquidity to make"veer off" coins on purported sidechains that can be "hued" toaddress any resource or responsibility, physical or computerized — a corporatestock or bond, a barrel of oil, a bar of gold, a vehicle, a vehicle installment, areceivable or a payable, or obviously a money. Sidechains areblockchains that have various elements and capabilities from thebitcoin blockchain however that influence bitcoin's laid out networkalso, equipment framework without reducing its securityhighlights. Sidechains interoperate with the blockchain through a twoway stake, a cryptographic method for moving resources off theblockchain and back again without an outsider trade. Othersstill are attempting to eliminate the coin or token out and out, buildingexchanging stages on private blockchains.

Monetary establishments arepreviously utilizing blockchain innovation to record, trade, and exchangeresources and liabilities, and could ultimately utilize it to supplantconventional trades and concentrated markets, overturning how wecharacterize and exchange esteem.Open Source: The monetary administrations industry is an innovation stackof inheritance frameworks standing twenty miles high and very nearlywavering over. Changes are hard to make in light of the fact that eachimprovement should be in reverse viable. As open sourceinnovation, blockchain can continually advance, repeat, andimprove, in view of agreement in the organization.These advantages — confirmation, decisively lower costs, lightning speed,lower chances, extraordinary development of significant worth, versatility — can possiblychange installments, yet additionally the protections business, speculationbanking, bookkeeping and review, investment, protection, endeavor riskthe board, retail banking, and different mainstays of the business.

"Money Road has awakened in a major way,"17 said Austin Slope of Blockstream.He was discussing the monetary business' profound interest in blockchainadvancements. Consider Blythe Experts, one of the most influential individuals onMoney Road. She incorporated JPMorgan's subsidiaries and wares work area into aworldwide juggernaut and spearheaded the subordinates market. After a briefpseudoretirement, she joined a New York-based fire up, Computerized ResourceProperty, as Chief. The choice astounded a large number. She comprehended that the blockchain would change her business as the Web changed otherbusinesses: "I would view it probably as in a serious way as you ought to have taken theidea of the Web during the 1990s. It's no joking matter and it will changethe way our monetary world operates."18Aces had excused a large number of the early stories of bitcoin, took advantage of bystreet pharmacists, tackled by players, and hailed by freedom supporters as making anew world request.

That changed in late 2014. Aces told us, "I had an 'ahasecond' where I started to see the value in the possible ramifications of theinnovation for the world that I knew well. While the cryptographic moneyutilization of the appropriated records innovation was intriguing and hadsuggestions for installments, the hidden information base innovation itself had farmore extensive implications."19 As per Experts, blockchain could decreaseshortcomings and expenses "by permitting various gatherings to depend on something very similardata as opposed to copying and reproducing it and having toaccommodate it." As a system for shared, decentralized, reproducedexchange records, blockchain is the "brilliant source," she says.20"Remember that monetary administrations foundations have not advanced inmany years. The front end has developed however not the back end," says Experts."It's been a weapons contest in innovation venture arranged toward speedingup exchange execution so that, these days, upper hands areestimated in parts of nanoseconds. The incongruity is that the posttradeframework hasn't exactly advanced by any stretch of the imagination." It actually takes "days and in somecases a long time of defer to do the posttrade handling that goes into in factsettling monetary exchanges and keeping record of them."21Aces isn't the only one in that frame of mind for blockchain innovation.NASDAQ Chief Bounce Greifeld said, "I'm a major devotee to the capacity ofblockchain innovation to impact basic change in the framework ofthe monetary assistance industry."22 Greifeld is incorporating blockchain'sappropriated record innovation into NASDAQ's confidential business sectors stagethrough a stage called NASDAQ Linq. Trades are brought togethercommercial centers for protections and they are additionally ready for disturbance.

On January1, 2016, NASDAQ Linq finished its most memorable exchange on blockchain. Concurringto Blockstream's Slope, one of the biggest resource chiefs on the planet "hasmore individuals committed to its blockchain development bunch than we have inour whole organization." Slope's organization has raised more than $75 million andutilizes in excess of twenty individuals. "These folks don't joke around about makingsure that they comprehend how they can utilize the innovation to change howthey do business."23 The NYSE, Goldman Sachs, Santander, Deloitte, RBC,Barclays, UBS, and essentially every major monetary firm worldwide have takena comparable serious interest. In 2015, Money Road's assessment of blockchaininnovation turned out to be all around certain: in one review, 94 percent ofrespondents said blockchain could assume a significant part in finance.24Albeit numerous different applications arouse the curiosity of Money Road,what intrigues monetary chiefs wherever is the idea of utilizing theblockchain to deal with any exchange safely from start to finish, whichcould decisively bring down costs, speed up and proficiency, and moderaterisk in their organizations. Aces said, "The whole life pattern of an exchangecounting its execution, the netting of different exchanges against one another, thecompromise of who did what with whom and whether they concur, canhappen at the exchange section level, significantly sooner in the heap of cycle, thanhappens in the standard monetary market."25 Greifeld put it along these lines: "Wepresently settle exchanges 'T+3' (that is, three days). Why not get comfortable five toten minutes?"26Money Road exchanges chance, and this innovation can physically diminishcounterparty risk, settlement chance, and subsequently fundamental gamble across the framework.Jesse McWaters, monetary advancement lead at the World Financial Discussion,told us, "The most interesting thing about circulated record innovation is the secretrecognizability can work on foundational dependability." He accepts these "new apparatusespermit controllers to utilize a lighter touch."27 The blockchain's public nature —its straightforwardness, its accessibility — in addition to its mechanized settlement andunchanging time stamps, permit controllers to see what's going on, even setup cautions so they don't miss anything.Banks and straightforwardness seldom remain inseparable. Most monetary entertainers gainupper hand from data deviations and more noteworthy expertise than their counterparties. Nonetheless, the bitcoin blockchain asdeveloped is a fundamentally straightforward framework. For banks, this implies openingthe kimono, in a manner of speaking. So how would we accommodate an open stage with theshut entryway strategy of banks?Austin Slope called it Money Road's "Faustian deal," a burdensome tradeoff.28 "Individuals genuinely want not holding up three days to settleexchanges yet having them cleared in practically no time and knowing thatthey're conclusive and that they're valid," said Slope. "The partner to that's it in a nutshellexchanges on the [bitcoin] blockchain are totally open.

That frightensvarious individuals on Money Road." The arrangement? Private exchangeson purported permissioned blockchains, otherwise called private blockchains.While the bitcoin blockchain is totally open and permissionless —

thatis, anybody can get to it and communicate with it — permissioned blockchainsexpect clients to have specific certifications, giving them a permit to work onthat specific blockchain. Slope has fostered the innovation by which as it werea couple of partners see the different parts of an exchange and canguarantee its trustworthiness.From the beginning, private and permissioned blockchains would appear toenjoy a couple of clear benefits. For one's purposes, its individuals can undoubtedly change therules of the blockchain assuming they so want. Expenses can be held down asexchanges need just approval from the actual individuals, eliminatingthe requirement for mysterious excavators who utilize bunches of power. Additionally, in light of the fact that allparties are trusted, a 51 percent assault is improbable. Hubs can be relied upon tobe very much associated, as in most use cases they are huge monetary organizations.Moreover, they are simpler for controllers to screen. Be that as it may, thesebenefits additionally make shortcomings. The simpler it is to change the standards, themore probable a part is to ridicule them. Private blockchains likewise forestall thenetwork impacts that empower an innovation to quickly scale. Purposefullyrestricting specific opportunities by making new principles can restrain nonpartisanship.At last, with no open worth development, the innovation is bound todeteriorate and become vulnerable.29 This isn't to say private blockchainswon't prosper, yet monetary administrations partners should in any case take theseconcerns genuinely.Swell Labs, which has gotten some momentum inside financial circles, iscreating other shrewd ways of alleviating Faust. "Swell Labs is focused ondiscount banking, and we utilize an agreement strategy, as opposed to a proof-ofwork framework," said President Chris Larsen, meaning no diggers and negativemysterious hubs are approving transactions.30 The organization Chain has itsown procedure. With $30 million in subsidizing from Visa, NASDAQ, Citi,Capital One, Fiserv, and Orange, Chain anticipates building enterprisefocused blockchain arrangements, focusing on the monetary administrations industry first,where it as of now has an arrangement with NASDAQ. "All resources later on will becomputerized carrier instruments running on numerous blockchains," contended ChainChief Adam Ludwin. Be that as it may, this will not be the siloed world Money Road isacquainted with, "in light of the fact that everybody is expanding on a similar open specs."31Wall Streeters should catch this innovation, however they shouldbattle with the worth advancement it empowers, something they have no control overor on the other hand foresee.Aces additionally sees the temperances of permissioned blockchains.

As far as she might be concerned, as it werea little cadre of exchanging accomplices, a few sellers and other counterparties,also, controllers need approach. Those limited handful picked will be allowedblockchain certifications. To Bosses, "permissioned records have thebenefit of never uncovering a managed monetary organization to the gamble ofeither executing with an obscure party, an unsatisfactory action from aadministrative perspective, or making a reliance upon an unexplored worldspecialist co-op like an exchange processor, additionally inadmissible from aadministrative mark of view."32 These permissioned blockchains, or privatechains, appeal to conventional monetary organizations careful about bitcoin andeverything related with it.While Blythe Bosses is the Chief of a beginning up, her strong fascinationaddresses more extensive association of conventional monetary entertainers in this area.This hug of new innovation mirrors a developing worry that tech new businesses can likewise overturn high money. For Eric Piscini of Deloitte, whose clientshave gone through an extraordinary arousing over the course of the last year, the "unexpected interestin tech was not something that anybody was expecting."33 The excitement isspreading like a virus into probably the biggest and most seasoned monetaryfoundations on the planet.Barclays is one of many monetary establishments investigatingpotential open doors in blockchain innovation. As indicated by Derek White,Barclays' central plan and computerized official, "advances like the blockchain are s in this industry. "We're quick to be shapers. But on the other hand we're quick toassociate with the shapers of the innovations and the interpreters of thoseadvancements," he said.34 Barclays is taking care of business,cutting huge number of occupations in customary regions and multiplying down oninnovation, prominently by sending off the Barclays Gas pedal. As indicated byWhite, "three out of the ten organizations in our last companion were blockchain orbitcoin organizations. Blockchain is the best proof of the world movingfrom shut frameworks to open frameworks and possibly affects thefate of monetary administrations as well as numerous industries."35 Banks talkingabout open frameworks.

5. Blockchain Technology and the Banking Industry

Blockchain innovation has been generally recognized as aproblematic power in the monetary area that is equipped for sabotagingcustomary plans of action and the advancements at present being used in a large numbermonetary help exchanges. This part centers around blockchain innovation's possible ramifications for the financial business. Expanding on theconsequences of a past report that I directed through subjective basedinterviews with three expert financiers from various European bankshandling the difficulties of blockchain, this part examines the expected benefits and dangers that blockchain innovation stances to banks andrecognizes the principal banking regions that can be affected.Blockchain innovation — alongside its fundamental applications, to be specific digital currencies and brilliant agreements — has drawn in a lot of considerationwhat's more, animated rich conversations among scholastics, experts and controllers all over the planet. It is presently recognized as a problematic powerin the monetary area and can subvert the customary plans of action and advancements that are presently utilized in many key monetary assistanceexchanges. As Philippon (2016, p. 2) notes, "such advancements canupset existing industry designs and obscure industry limits, work withkey disintermediation, reform how existing firms make andconvey items and administrations, give new passages to business venture,democratize admittance to monetary administrations, yet additionally make critical security,administrative and policing".Concerning banking industry specifically, the developing revenue inblockchain innovation results from its capacity to set out new open doorsfor banks and to present new dangers to their business, as it might move alongthe effectiveness of the cycles basic the monetary administrations offer,subsequently encouraging the proposal of more excellent administrations. It might likewise permit thepassage of new administrators with a resulting extension of the cutthroatsetting.

Nonetheless, similar to any arising innovation, blockchain's true capacitysuggestions are both expansive and not yet completely comprehended.To reveal insight into the ramifications of blockchain innovation in thebanking area, this part tries to make sense of (1) the likely advantages, aswell as dangers, that blockchain may model for banks and (2) the principal bankingregions that might be impacted by the reception of this innovation. Thepart depends on the consequences of a past report I directed throughsubjective based interviews with three expert brokers in variousEuropean banks that are managing the difficulties of blockchain with respect to blockchain's expected ramifications for banks, it is worthnoticing that the original blockchain (Blockchain 1.0.) — that is,blockchain used to help Bitcoin (and other cryptocurrencies)3 — was at first planned as a stage for disintermediation (Martino 2019). Itsprimary design was to make an electronic installment framework to permit thedirect exchange of significant worth between two gatherings without the requirement for a trustedoutsider (a focal power or a mediator like a bank). Disintermediation implies the blockchain connected to digital forms of money disposes of theneed for go-betweens, for example, banks since it empowers people andassociations to execute and manufacture arrangements straightforwardly with each otherwithout chances. Along these lines, banks are not generally expected to confirm the gatherings'characters, lay out trust or perform basic exercises like the contracting,clearing, settling and record-keeping of undertakings (McDonald et al. 2016;Holotiuk et al. 2017; Iansiti and Lakhani 2017).In principle, original blockchain represents a danger to the bankingindustry since blockchain and Bitcoin (as well as other digital currencies), taken together, are devices for disintermediating banks. Concurringto McDonald et al. (2016), blockchain can be viewed as another institutional innovation that would re-request the administration of the creationof banking administrations since it empowers bank exchanges to create some distance fromunified various leveled associations towards a decentralized market.Today, moving worth in a last way requires a long cycle withvarious players (for example clients, banks, clearing frameworks, settlementframeworks, etc) dealing with a Quick network,4 which banks useto move a wide range of monetary data. To really move cash,a few concentrated frameworks go about as a "legal official" of the exchange, making itan extremely lengthy and complex interaction.

By means of blockchain, related toBitcoin (and other cryptographic forms of money), this cycle can happen in aimmediate, secure and "last" way without the contribution of the playersreferenced previously. In particular, attributable to the critical qualities of thedisseminated record innovation (see Part 2), blockchain connected to digital currencies causes it feasible for two individuals who to don't have the foggiest idea about one anotherto straightforwardly trade computerized resources in a safe and "last" way. This impliesthat, toward the finish of the exchange, there is a compelling possession move(Martino 2019).In view of the contemplations above, original blockchain can beconsidered another player that rivals banks, since blockchain and cryptographic forms of money work with new devices that can be sent to deal with thehardships of executing (MacDonald et al. 2016; Lindman et al. 2017;Outline et al. 2018), and they offer huge benefits over banks ina few regions (for example installments) by permitting a quick, minimal expense and secure wayto move esteem. These benefits, as made sense of above, are relatedwith the end of middle people in exchanges and the resulting banking charges. Moreover, new blockchain-based new businesses (for examplealleged fintech organizations) may arise and offer some financial administrationswith lower charges, subsequently possibly making banks lose their piece of the pie(Philippon 2016; Stulz 2019). For example, numerous fintech new businesses aredynamic today in sections of the worth chain that are now overseen bybanks, for example, business and shopper loaning (PwC 2020). Such firmsinfluence blockchain innovation to offer attributes and subsidizing to people and organizations with lower exchange costs; accordingly, they rivalcustomary business banks. Along these lines, blockchain and cryptographic forms of money might risk one of the financial area's center business exercises (for exampleloaning), with the ensuing disintegration of bank income, in this manner sabotagingthe banks' benefit (Yeoh 2017). As per Gartner (2018), oneof the world's driving exploration and warning organizations, 80% of legacymonetary administrations firms will leave business by 2030, become commoditised or exist just officially without contending successfully. The justification forthis is that worldwide computerized stages, fintech organizations and different playerswill acquire more noteworthy portion of the overall industry by utilizing arising advances, for example,blockchain, to change the business' monetary and plans of action.

Today, the biggest banks recognize the potential dangers presented bythis new contender. In its yearly 10-K recording with the Protections andTrade Commission (SEC) delivered in February 2019, the Bankof America Organization (BofA) recorded digital currencies among the gamblefactors that could affect the bank's intensity anddiminish its incomes and benefits. BofA announced that mechanical advances(like digital currencies) bring empowered new players to the table for items andadministrations that had generally been banking items, as well as new imaginative items, at a lower cost, in this way expanding contest, which,thusly, may hurt bank profit through a few channels. For example,BofA calls attention to that these new advancements make strain on banks tobring down the costs of — or the credit principles applied to — their itemswhat's more, administrations, require significant uses to change or adjust existingitems and administrations to remain cutthroat and influence the ability of clients to work with banks. This can decrease banks' net revenue edge and incomes from their expense based items and administrations.This view is additionally upheld by the enormous US bank JPMorgan Pursue, whichrecognized in its yearly 10-K documenting that installment handling and otherbanking administrations could be essentially disturbed by new advancementslike digital currencies.

It called attention to how these advances require thatbanks make extra speculations for them to stay serious andcan come down on the evaluating of banks' items and administrations or causethe bank to lose portion of the overall industry, especially to the extent that conventional bankingitems like stores and ledgers are concerned. As indicated byJPMorgan Pursue, any such effect could lessen the bank's incomes andbenefit.Regardless, the potential dangers referenced above don't represent anquick danger to banks, since the utilization of blockchain connected todigital forms of money is compelled by a few limits: there are variousadministrative issues (connected to illegal exercises like tax evasion, psychological oppressorfunding and tax avoidance), specialized/versatility issues, plan of actionchallenges, government decides and others that as of now limit the utilization of thissort of blockchain and alleviate the related dangers for banks (Martino2019).Guideline issues are among the main issues restricting theuse of blockchain connected to digital forms of money at present since thebanking area is exceptionally controlled, while blockchain and digital currencies are, generally, not (yet). For example, for issues connected withpsychological warfare and duty aversion, among others, banks should follow exchangesbit by bit, which isn't generally achievable with original blockchain,hence

71

raising issues connected with exchange detectability. As Houben andSnyers (2018) contend, digital currencies are believed to be truly reasonable forillegal exercises given their secrecy, cross-line nature and fast adaptability.

A frequently proposed illustration of where blockchain can be applied to get to the next levelprocess effectiveness are clearing and settlement frameworks, which at presentrequire a perplexing cycle with numerous players, heap messages andmanual compromises and are, hence, described by significant time frames(Buithenek 2016; Fanning and Focuses 2016; Peters and Panayi 2016).Blockchain innovation might give a superior clearing and settlementframework by permitting banks to clear and settle straightforwardly and safely, accordinglylessening functional expenses and timing for exercises like corporate loaningfurthermore, capital business sectors. As indicated by an Accenture Counseling (2017) study,enormous venture banks could save $10 billion by utilizing blockchain innovation to work on the productivity of clearing and settlement, which areright now overseen by means of a large group of messages and manual compromises.Subsequently, exercises like protections exchanges, where post-exchange clearingwhat's more, settlement is slow and costly and includes many gatherings, maybenefit from the reception of blockchain (Yermack 2019), which cansafely and straightforwardly move protections right away or minutes, withprogrammed clearing and settlement (Buithenek 2016). As a result,this would prompt decreased expenses and lower counterparty risk relatedwith clearing and settlement (McKinsey and Company 2016). A few exchanges affect capital business sectors.

For example, in April 2019, Société Générale SFH, an auxiliary of SociétéGénérale Gathering, gave e100 million in covered bonds as a security tokenstraightforwardly enrolled on the Ethereum blockchain, investigating a more proficientprocess for bond issuances by diminishing expenses and the quantity of delegates included. Accordingly, in September 2019, Banco Santandergiven the principal start to finish blockchain bond (worth \$20 million) utilizing3 BLOCKCHAIN Innovation AND THE Financial Business 41the public Ethereum blockchain, which permitted the bank to tokenise thebond safely (for example carefully address customary resources on the blockchain)furthermore, register it in a permissioned way on the blockchain.

The mechanization of the whole interaction empowered the bank to lessen the quantity ofmediators expected simultaneously, making the exchange quicker,less complex and more proficient.One more movement in this space covers partnered credits, which take onnormal something like 20 days for an exchange to be settled by the banksbecause of the amount of data traded, extended surveys and thepaper types of correspondence between parties (Fanning and Focuses2016). Blockchain might decrease the time and expenses for the exchangevia mechanizing the whole cycle and making it more straightforward. To begin with,at the point when a party enters contract data into the blockchain, data is made accessible continuously to any remaining gatherings, subsequently eliminating theneed for paper correspondences and numerous agreement audits. Additionally, shrewdagreements can be utilized to digitize the partnered advance to accommodate exchangesagainst credit arrangements, naturally charge interest installments fromthe borrower's record and change credit obligation inside the blockchain.As Rutenberg and Wenner (2017) propose, by utilizing shrewd reaches, itis feasible to deal with the whole interaction — from going into the advanceagreement and gathering interest installments to calling a default and evenholding onto guarantee — with practically no human inclusion.

This can diminish theneed for manual compromises and handling, which can bring about timefurthermore, cost reserve funds. For example, in 2018, Spain's BBVA and two accomplicebanks (MUFG of Japan and BNP Paribas of France) finished the firstpartnered credit (to the tune of e150 million) on blockchain with theRed Eléctrica company, in this way giving a functioning illustration of how suchexchanges can be improved and advanced quickly by utilizing blockchain innovation. The entire discussion process was finished over a private blockchainnetwork, which altogether facilitated the cycle while guaranteeing fulldocumentation following and discussion straightforwardness.

Blockchain may likewise emphatically influence exchange finance, a business region portrayed by significant expenses and low proficiency in light of the fact that many cycles includebroad manual investigations, paper-based exchanges (for example letters ofcredit) and various middle people.42 P. MARTINOGrinding in worldwide business sectors makes getting supporting and finishingexchanges an extensive and complex interaction that incorporates different exercises suchas loaning, giving letters of credit, figuring and safeguarding the gatherings(Lang 2017).

Monetary organizations are expected to make credit appraisals and perform installments — frequently through paper-based trade andapproval of records — across different members (FBS 2019). Ingeneral, it can require days to weeks to finish a solitary exchange.Blockchain innovation can assist with lightening these gratings in exchange bydecreasing the broad measure of documentation and complex reportstreams included (Cong and He 2019; Yermack 2019). By utilizing blockchaininnovation to digitalise and validate records (for example by means of shrewd agreements)furthermore, permitting the gatherings associated with an activity to get to a similar data, it is feasible to lessen time, cost and functional gamble (Buithenek2016; Guo and Liang 2016).

This implies that blockchain may empowermembers from various areas (for example banking and cargo transporting) tostraightforwardly collaborate and share data in an all the more effectively evident anddecentralized way to speed up exchanges and lessenthe requirement for paper compromise (FSB 2019). For example, in May2018, HSBC and ING Bank finished the world's first industriallysuitable exchange finance exchange for the worldwide food and agribusiness combination Cargill by utilizing blockchain (explicitly, R3's adaptableCorda blockchain stage). HSBC gave a letter of credit to ING forthe firm Cargill and executed the exchange in a record season of 24 hoursrather than the standard time of 5-10 days by eliminating the requirement forpaper compromise, since all gatherings were connected on the stage andrefreshed immediately.3.3.3 Installment FrameworksAnother financial region that could profit from the reception of blockchainadvancements covers installments frameworks, which would mean moving pieces ofbanks' installment frameworks to blockchain innovation so it might work withquicker installments at lower costs. Right now, esteem move is costly andslow, especially in cross-line installments, in light of a progression of confounded processes (for example manual compromise) and the requirement for go-betweenclearing firms. A solitary installment exchange frequently includes a criticalnumber of gatherings and is regularly helped out through decentralized andcomplex reporter banking networks that face difficulties connecting withcost and client a reasonable level of effort, as well as shortcomings from tasks3 BLOCKCHAIN Innovation AND THE Financial Business 43across various monetary standards, message designs, time regions and regulations (FSB2019). For instance, sending $100 from a country in Europe to a country(all things considered, five)days for handling.Blockchain innovation might make it conceivable to acknowledge installmentsimmediately and decrease exchange failure via computerizing compromise,lessening functional expenses or expanding the accessibility of "know-yourcustomer" (KYC) information. In particular, by applying blockchain innovation toinstallments, exchanges can be executed straightforwardly between banks withoutany outsider, accordingly working on the interaction and offering many benefits to banks, like lower exchange and functional expenses, alsoas sped up (Buithenek 2016; Fanning and Focuses2016; Guo and Liang 2016).

As indicated by gauges by Deloitte (2016),business-to-business and one individual to the next installments across borders withblockchain may bring about a 40-80%

decrease in exchange costs andtake a normal of four to six seconds to conclude, rather than the normmove interaction of a few days. In April 2018, Banco Santandersent off the first blockchain-based worldwide cash move administration,which makes it feasible for clients to finish global exchangesaround the same time or quite soon. It likewise shows the specific sum thatclients will get in the objective cash before they make themove.3.3.4 ConsistenceVia robotizing parts of banks' business processes, blockchain may likewisealtogether decrease the expenses related with regions like consistence, whichare portrayed by profoundly manual and paper-based processes that leadto postponements, failures and expanded openness to mistakes and misrepresentation(Capgemini Counseling 2016).The weight of giving controllers an ever increasing number of information aroundthe world is a tedious undertaking for the monetary organizations and controllers who need to deal with such huge measures of data. Blockchaincould altogether decrease the expenses related with such tasks. Itmay improve on all regulatory work associated with the consistence cyclesince with blockchain an exchange is programmed, and afterward it consequentlytakes care of the consistence information base. For example, Buithenek (2016) proposesthat blockchain, by empowering shrewd agreements, could make it conceivable toimplement consistence forthright as opposed to checking it after an exchange,44   P.   MARTINOconsequently   decisively lessening the time and exertion that monetary foundations spend on administrative revealing and working on the quality, precisionalso, speed of the whole interaction. Accordingly, it will likewise lessen the expensesinvolved.

This implies that consistence can work progressively concerningthe installment cycle (and, as a rule, any financial movement), work on thespeed of cycles and lessen the connected expenses. Besides, blockchainmight be utilized to monitor the means that guidelines require: permanentlyrecording exchanges on the disseminated record, which renders data decentralized and open, gives an exhaustive, securewhat's more, irreversible monetary review trail for controllers to check consistence,accordingly dispensing with the requirement for controllers to gather, store, accommodate andtotal data. By permitting controllers and national banks to autonomously separate data on exchanges, banks might stay away from all theauthoritative work, which diminishes the need to effectively gather, confirm andconvey information (for example sending great many reports) (Auer 2019).3.3.5 Know Your ClientUtilizing blockchain to share data about clients may likewise get to the next levelthe proficiency of know-your-client (KYC) processes by diminishingthe pointless duplication of data and solicitations (Lang 2017;Moyano and Ross 2017).The KYC interaction comprises of a trade of records between theclient and the monetary foundation to gather clients' essential personalitydata (Moyano and Ross 2017). Such cycles in numerous monetaryfoundations are wasteful and portrayed by significant time frames, the duplication of exertion and a potential for blunder, which are expensive and couldadditionally hurt clients' insight (Capgemini 2019). A worldwide overview byThomson Reuters (2016) reports that the expenses and intricacy of KYCare rising, and monetary foundations are spending between $60 million and$500 million every year to stay aware of KYC and client an expected level of investmentguidelines.Blockchain's disseminated record innovation can accelerate the KYCinteraction and make it safer and proficient.

Through its cryptographicassurance, which assists with keeping data secure, and its capacity toshare a continually refreshed record with many gatherings, blockchain mayguarantee predictable and solid client data. This implies that onceclients do the full KYC process with one bank, datacoming about because of the KYC cycle might be imparted to different banks, which3 BLOCKCHAIN Innovation AND THE Financial Business 45will kill excess work and decrease the quantity of steps in currentKYC rehearses. Generally, blockchain may empower the production of aordered, decentralized and shared information safe in which banksthat need to lead KYC rehearses for a client can straightforwardly check theaftereffect of the cycle that has proactively been led for this client,in this manner staying away from copy KYC assignments and accomplishing cost and time reserve funds.

This might prompt an expansion in effectiveness in the wide sense, both aslower expenses and time to do KYC processes and on the grounds that the clienthas the quick advantage of opening a record, in contrast to other currentframeworks. For sure, from a client viewpoint, blockchain can diminish onboarding stand by times and dispose of the need to give the equivalent over and overdata to their monetary administrations suppliers (KPMG 2018).Taken together, the contemplations above are especially fascinatingconcerning banks' likely benefit. In the event that banks can consolidate thisinnovation into their plans of action and lift their productivity in wordingof cost decreases, they might diminish the commissions they charge theirclients and have a superior edge, since the diminishing in the commissionsmight be adjusted by the decline in costs. Hence, blockchain can be instrumental in working on the nature of the administrations proposed to clients, whichwill give a significant upper hand. Regardless, it is worthtaking note of that, until this point, there has not been any proof of blockchain innovation utilization prompting proficiency upgrades (for example cost decreases).It will require a few years before blockchain demonstrates that it worksactually and can produce benefits for banks (Martino 2019).Moreover, a few issues should be tended to before blockchain mayuncover every one of the advantages referenced previously.

Notwithstanding enhancements in financial cycles' effectiveness, a furtheradvantage of blockchain for banks is admittance to bunches of data. Havingrecorded on the conveyed record a full and straightforward history that anyclient banks have ready, blockchain may give an approach to banks toacquire quick and secure admittance to refreshed client information, coming about in more prominentfunctional proficiency and a decrease in the time and cost expected toassemble and handle information.Information is a vital source to develop data that can give thefirm with an upper hand (Prescott 2016). Since dataon client installments and credit profiles addresses a wellspring of information about clients for banks, banks might use this data as asecret weapon to create new items and administrations to betteraddress client needs (Martino 2019). By and by, the critical benefitfor banks is the capacity to get to various and expanded sorts of data — relating not exclusively to the bank (for example data on clients)yet additionally to different associations like boats, ports, etc and theircoming about abuse — to make new items and administrations that don'texist yet. The accessibility of a progression of conveyed data got from different sources provides saves money with a superior and more complete comprehension of their clients' ways of behaving, necessities and inclinations (Prescott2016), which empowers banks to make and offer items and administrationscustom-made to these clients' singular necessities.Subsequently, making new items and administrations by using data onthe blockchain may create major new income streams for banks andmight be critical to acquiring an upper hand (Vermeulen 2004; Accenture2016).About 1.7 billion people today don't have a record with amonetary organization (Demirguc-Kunt et al. 2018).

They comprise whathas been known as the unbanked populace, while numerous othershave restricted admittance to conventional monetary administrations and are known as theunderbanked population.7 Together, these gatherings represent exactly 2billion monetarily avoided people worldwide.8 Besides, over halfthe miniature, little and average sized endeavors (MSMEs) in developing business sectors,equalling in excess of 200 million organizations, right now don't approachto banking administrations (EY 2017).These people face hardships getting to banking administrations for a fewreasons. To begin with, banks experience issues contacting these people due totheir unfortunate records of loan repayment and the absence of proper distinguishing proof requiredto open a financial balance, for instance, which makes it hard to executeKYC rehearses and other qualification and a reasonable level of effort prerequisites toofficially open a record. Unexpected issues connect with the moderatenessof monetary items and administrations, lacking installment and credit frameworks, the restricted geological admittance to monetary establishments, etc(Natarajan et al. 2017; Lichtfous et al. 2018).New innovations can work with more productive admittance to this market,successfully making the expenses and benefits in serving this portion moreappealing (Ouma et al. 2017; EY 2017). This area of the planet populacemay address a critical chance for banks since blockchain innovationcould permit them to get to banking administrations significantly more easily.Thus, with blockchain, banks might reach unbanked and underbankedpeople by tending to their requirements and tackling the greater part of the previously mentioned difficulties (Natarajan et al. 2017; Lichtfous et al. 2018; Schuetzalso, Venkatesh 2020). In the first place, banks can contact these people by permittingthem to make their own monetary other options (for example cryptographic forms of money) thatmeet explicit client needs at a reasonable expense (EY 2017). The benefit can come from involving the advanced cash as the exchange mediumbetween two gatherings universally (for example as an all inclusive method for trade),which brings down exchange costs by keeping people from payingcash expenses when they move cash to various nations. Since theyare all inclusive monetary forms, digital currencies wipe out the unfamiliar tradeexchange expenses that banks normally charge. Second, inferable from the innovation's capacity to lay out a computerized personality quickly and cost-successfully,blockchain may empower banks to take care of issues connected to KYC processeswhile attempting to serve these possible clients, accordingly permitting the monetaryconsideration of already underserved customer portions.These contemplations recommend that blockchain may open new marketportions for existing banks and permit them to arrive at numerous new possible clients, subsequently producing new income streams and getting to the next leveltheir productivity. As indicated by Accenture (2015) gauges, by bringingthe present avoided people and organizations — especially those in thebigger and more prosperous developing business sector districts — into the formalbanking area banks could create about $380 billion every year in newincomes.

This view is additionally upheld by ongoing exploration directed byEY (2017), which shows that banks can drive comprehensive development, reestablishtrust and lift benefits by serving underbanked people and organizationsin developing business sectors. In particular, EY (2017) gauges that banks couldproduce steady yearly income of $200 billion by better servingmonetarily prohibited people and MSMEs in 60 arising nations. This section shed light on blockchain's possible ramifications for banks.It is vital to separate between blockchain innovation connectedto digital forms of money (for example original blockchain) and blockchain'sappropriated record innovation (for example second-age blockchain). Whileblockchain connected to digital forms of money is seen as a likely danger tobanks in light of the fact that blockchain and cryptographic forms of money address a device to disintermediate banks, blockchain's dispersed record innovation (especially private or permissioned blockchain) gives an open door since it mightfurther develop banking cycles' effectiveness and the administrations that banks proposition totheir clients, with a positive effect on banks' benefit. Loaning,installment frameworks, exchange money and capital market are the fundamental bankingregions that could profit from taking on blockchain innovation. Also,blockchain may empower banks to make new item and administrations andto arrive at new clients from among the unbanked and underbankedpopulaces, hence possibly producing major new income streams.

Despite the fact that blockchain is two-sided, it as of now presents an open doorfor as opposed to a gamble to banks on the grounds that the utilization of blockchain connected todigital forms of money is hampered by a few administrative and specialized issuesthat right now diminish the possible dangers to banks. On the other hand, bankscan take advantage of the advantages of blockchain's conveyed record innovation byintegrating the innovation into their plans of action.

6. Creation of Digital Coins

Bitcoin, the main digital currency, didn't simply unexpectedly show up. Numerous of the innovations it is based on are as old as the actual web. The roots of cryptographic amounts of money and basic blockchain innovation dive deep into a community of programmers, activists, and technologists who still impact the turn of events what's more, the course of digital currencies, and the web in general, today. A fundamental apparatus inside bitcoin is advanced cryptography. This essential part of the web is available in everything from WiFi to email, computerized shopping baskets to Mastercard. W without cryptography to keep data hidden on the web, there would be no web as far as we might be concerned. Also, without cryptography, digital currencies couldn't work. Advanced cryptographic devices have for some time been the region o characters on the edges of society: programmers and spies. From the outset look these two gatherings probably won't appear to have much in common, however, both offer a requirement for outright security. Between the two shafts of programmers and spies lies the dull web —the part of the web stowed away from curious eyes by encryption. The dim web pushes the limit of what is conceivable, to what is legitimate. It is here that the thought of digital currency was conceived. Without a doubt, it could never have been developed elsewhere. In the 1970s a U S nonconformist gathering called hippies, driven by dissident Abbie Hoffman started distributing a pamphlet that educated, among different stunts, how to take administration from phone specialist organizations. W cap started as an enemy of power motion and developed into something else. Self-depicted 'programmers' started testing to see precisely the way that far they could break into innovative frameworks without getting found out. In any case, when innovation developed and telephone lines became information lines, this investigation became more serious. Activities once considered tricks or harmless burglaries before long turned out to be genuine disturbances. In 1988, a PC worm that would come to be called the Morris Worm started repeating itself across PCs by means of the web.

Oneself repeating malware's expectation wasn't to break anything, but just to spread to the furthest extent that it would be able. However, in the process of doing as such, it crashed numerous frameworks. The U S specialists didn't find this analysis entertaining. Robert Morris, a graduate understudy and maker of the Morris Worm, turned into thefirst individual indicted under the PC Extortion and MisuseRepresent deliberately getting to government PCs (where his work in the end wound up) without approval, and for causing significant harm.As the web was created and PCs turned out to be progressively arranged, programmers faced more legal snags.During the 1990s, legislatures all over the planet started to take activity, endeavoring to tame the uncivilized web. Accordingly, segments of the PC people group took neutralization. Some were spurred by freedom advocates and rebel methods of reasoning, joined together by their general doubt of government. Others, perceiving how regulation implementation organizations could aggrieve the individuals who didn't mean any genuine mischief, started coordinating to shield revolutionary programmers and consistently PC clients the same. In 1990, the Electronic Outskirts Establishment was made because of the continuous PCerime crackdown.This non-profit association still exists today, giving legitimate insight and activism on a wide assortment of privacy issues. Be that as it may, PC clients required more than legal advisors to protect themselves against the public authority s move into the web. They required new innovation.The mid-1990s brought forth the 'cypherpunk' — a sort of programmer whose bread and butter was computerized cryptography. The cypherpunks didn't zero in on breaking into PC frameworks.

Rather, they created instruments that made a cover o electronic security on the web. The most important device developed from a disclosure by researchers W hitfield D iffie and Martin Hellm an of every 19 7 6. T h eyfigured out a method of asymmetric encryption that permitted two individuals to com -m unicate furtively, without truly trading a codebook. In 19 9 1, adjusting this method to modern times, programmer and against atomic dissident Phil Zim m erm unfostered a program called Pretty God P privacy (PG P) and transferred the source code to the web where anybody could unload it and send scrambled messages for free.T he cypherpunks were happy. T h e programming worked so well for keeping correspondence secret that the U S government attempted to indict Zimmerman for 'sending out an m munition: an infringement of regulations endeavoring to keep innovation with high military worth from leaving the country.After one year, in September 1992, a web-based mailing list was sent off under the name Cypherpunk. The discussion drew in all sorts of individuals keen on utilizing innovation to keep up with their protection, and included such devices as PGP, remailing administrations that clouded an email source s genuine location, and theoretical thoughts, for example, 'untraceable' computerized cash. Around then, with the public authority after Zimmerman, it was not satisfied that encryption would be legitimate over the long haul. The Cypherpunk list, hence, pulled in individuals keen on security as well as those able to wander into the dim regions of the law to safeguard their protection. The cypherpunks thought it likely that in the event that they didn't push the mechanical envelope, the new web would be utilized altogether for observation, and individual security may be lost until the end of time. They started to think about their activities, similar to those of Zimmerman, to be considerate defiance — delivering data to people in general for a long-term benefit, in any case, of what the public authority said was lawful. Virtual cash advocates were on the Cypherpunk list alone. Hal Finney, who dealt with PGP with Phil Zimmerman, was on the rundown and would later be one o the first to assist Satoshi Nakamoto with working on the bitcoin source code. Someone else on the rundown was Adam Back, who utilized cryptography to foster a spam decrease device called 'hash cash', which he imparted to the Cypherpunk email list in 1997.

Likewise on the rundown were cryptographer N yuck Szabo who explored different avenues regarding virtual money of his own, called Piece Gold, and Craig Wright, an

Australian engaged with different security innovations, including those getting financial exchanges. Ali o these names would be significant in the future of bitcoin and digital forms of money. In 2008, Satoshi Nakamoto freely declared his thoughts on digital money he called 'bitcoin' on a replacement mailing list to Cypherpunk's unique email list. Albeit many were at first incredulous about bitcoin's efficacy, Nakamoto had found the best crowd to see the value in his idea. In any case, cypherpunks are just around 50% of the set of experiences of the dull web. The other half comes from an instrument created by the U S specialists to safeguard their government operatives.

Printed in the USA
CPSIA information can be obtained
at www.ICGtesting.com
LVHW091049060524
779122LV00009B/1048